THE
SECOND BIRTH
Love Wisdom Truth

Translated from the French
Original title: LA DEUXIÈME NAISSANCE
Amour Sagesse Vérité

Original edition:
© 1974, Éditions Prosveta S.A. (Suisse)

Prosveta S.A – B.P.12 – 83601 Fréjus CEDEX (France)
ISBN 978-2-85566-441-5

Omraam Mikhaël Aïvanhov

THE
SECOND BIRTH
Love Wisdom Truth

Complete Works – Volume 1

P R O S V E T A

Readers will better understand certain aspects of the lectures published in the present volume if they bear in mind that Master Omraam Mikhaël Aïvanhov's teaching was exclusively oral and that the editors have made every effort to respect the flavour and style of each lecture.

The Master's teaching is more than a body of doctrines; it is an organic whole, and his way of presenting it was to approach it from countless different points of view. By treating certain aspects in many different contexts he constantly reveals a new dimension of the whole, and at the same time throws new light on the individual aspects and their vital links with each other.

Omraam Mikhaël Aïvanhov

TABLE OF CONTENTS

Chapter One

THE SECOND BIRTH

If you were to visit the Brotherhood in Bulgaria when the brothers and sisters are camping up in the mountains, near the seven lakes of Rila, you would see a natural spring not far from the camp, that has been arranged as a unique kind of fountain. The water flows from a huge block of stone carved in the shape of a ship's prow, from which it runs down onto a bed of very white, flat stones and pours out between two carved hands. All who wish can drink from this source of pure, fresh water flowing from the two hands. On the rock to the left of the spring, is the symbol of the Brotherhood: an engraving of an anchor, painted in red, and on the right is the following inscription:

Brothers and sisters,
Father and mothers,
Friends and strangers,
Teachers and students,
All you who are the servants of life,
Be like this spring:
Open your hearts to good!

There are also some geometrical figures and cabbalistic symbols carved beside this text; but I will talk to you about them another time.

You are all familiar with the passage in the Gospel of St John in which Jesus tells Nicodemus, *'Very truly, I tell you, no one can see the kingdom of God without being born anew.'* Nicodemus, who was astounded by this, asked, *'How can anyone be born after having grown old? Can one enter a second time into the mother's womb and be born?'* And Jesus replied, *'Very truly, I tell you, no one can enter the kingdom of God without being born of water and Spirit.'* What does *'being born of water and Spirit'* mean?

In very ancient times, in the city of Jerusalem, lived a sage by the name of Nathan. When the Sultan Saladin captured the city, he heard tell of Nathan and commanded that he be brought before him. Saladin asked this wise man seven questions, and one of them was this: 'Which is the most perfect religion: Judaism, Buddhism, Christianity or Muhammadanism?' Nathan replied, 'I'll tell you a story. There was once a king who possessed a magic ring which made him all-powerful, and thanks to this magic power, his kingdom was never troubled by war, disease or disaster. Now the king had three sons who were all equally dear to him and, when he felt that he was getting old, he could not make up his mind which son should inherit his ring. Then he thought of a solution; he called the court goldsmith to him and told him to make two copies of the magic ring. This he did, and, when the king shuffled the three rings together, they were so alike that even he could not tell which was the original. Then the king called each of his sons to him in turn and said the same thing to each of them: 'My son, I love you very dearly; I am going to give you a third of my kingdom and, in secret, you shall also have my magic ring.' The king himself did not know which son had received the magic ring, but each of them was convinced that he had it.

Some months went by, and the king decided to go and visit his sons. He went, first of all, to the kingdom of his eldest son and, when he saw that his subjects suffered from poverty and disease, he knew that it was not he who had received the magic ring.

Next, he went to visit the second son, and there, too, he found the population afflicted by war and endless misfortunes: the magic ring was not there, either. Finally, when he reached the kingdom of his third son, he found that all his subjects were prosperous and healthy and lived in peace and happiness. Then the king understood that it was his youngest son who had inherited the magic ring. And that', said Nathan; 'is how you will know which is the true religion: the one in which peace, happiness, prosperity, wisdom and love reign.'

If, in spite of the teaching received from the great masters, we have still not discovered truth, it may well be because the channels within us are blocked up and the currents cannot circulate. This is something I understood when I was still very young. Let me tell you how: I studied hard, read a great deal and worked continuously, and yet I was never really satisfied. So then, one day, I decided to fast. I fasted for ten days and, after that, I understood a great many things that I had never found in books. To begin with I felt famished, but that feeling did not last very long. On the third or fourth day I was terribly thirsty and this got worse and worse during the following days. When I slept, I dreamed that I was drinking from springs and rivers but that my thirst still was not quenched. And then, one day, I was no longer thirsty. On the seventh day I picked up a piece of fruit and inhaled its perfume, and the essence emanating from it was so extraordinarily subtle and strong that I felt nourished by it and, for the last two or three days, the only food and drink I needed were these subtle emanations. This was how I learned that each plant, each fruit contains its own subtle, etheric elements, but that we are too well-fed and replete to be able to perceive or benefit from them. So many things exist all around us, but we are too 'full' to receive them! Precious though they may be, we have to suffer real hunger and thirst before being aware that they exist;[1] we are somnolent and unaware like those who habitually overeat, and this is why we are deprived of certain subtler foods.

Someone who habitually overeats becomes so clogged up that he becomes drowsy, sluggish and comatose. His senses lose their finer edge, his intelligence is clouded, his will is sapped and his passions become coarser and more demanding. And the same is true on other planes. If you 'eat' too much on the astral plane, the subtler elements of the soul and of nature will escape you; they will be beyond the perception of your consciousness. And in these conditions, of course, even if all the greatest masters of humanity came to teach you their wisdom, you would neither understand nor feel any of it. This is what my fast taught me, for I found that astral projection was so much easier when I was not eating: I could leave my body and travel to subtler regions with the greatest of ease, whereas, when I began eating normally again, it became much more difficult.

The little spring of water murmurs, 'Be like me! Be alive; flow!' Yes, if you refuse to take the spring of living water as your model, you will become a stagnant bog. If your inner spring ceases to flow, fermentation and rot will set in. And you know what that means: you will be infested by mosquitoes, flies and every kind of vermin, and nothing you can do will get rid of them again; they will continue to proliferate. The only solution is to drain the bog and allow the spring waters to flow freely once more. There is no danger of putrefaction in the presence of a free-flowing spring.[2] On the contrary, you all know what happens: trees grow tall, flowers blossom and the birds sing. You will ask, 'What do I have to do for this inner spring to start flowing in me?' It is very simple: all you have to do is to love. Oh, yes, I know... You will say that you already love, that everybody loves... That is true, but I am speaking of another kind of love. Most people would admit that being in love was a painful experience and that it made them miserable, but this only means that what they experienced was not really love. The kind of love that makes someone miserable is not true love: it is a malady! And the strange thing is that almost no one is immune to it. It is a raging epidemic: however many precautions you take, you end up by catching it and being ravaged by it.

I once had a friend in Bulgaria who used to talk about love as the most beautiful thing in the world. One day he came to see me, his hair tangled and unkempt, gloom and desolation written in every line of his features. When I anxiously asked what was wrong with him, he replied, 'I'm in love, that's all!' His love made him very unhappy because he could not possess the object of his affections. But true love, the love I am talking about is something completely different: when we are in possession of this true love, the love that this new teaching is all about, we cannot help but be happy because it is a glorious state of consciousness which brings with it all blessings. As soon as a spring begins to flow within us, trees, flowers, animals and men also appear, for a culture always grows up alongside running water; in other words, vegetation, animals and human civilization always flourish in the presence of true love.[3]

Can we give another interpretation to this? Yes: the mineral kingdom represents our bones; the vegetable kingdom represents our muscular system; the animal kingdom represents our circulatory system, and the kingdom of men represents our nervous system.

'No one can see the kingdom of God without being born of water and Spirit.' What are the water and the spirit? In Esoteric Science, water has always been seen as the passive element whereas the spirit, on the contrary, is an active principle. In Hebrew, the word for water is maim and the word for spirit is *ruah*. The curious thing about this word is that, if you say it in reverse it becomes *haur,* and this means light, the light that created the world. *Haur* is the light that lives in every human soul as a tiny spark of the creative masculine principle, celestial fire. Whereas water is the passive feminine principle, the plastic medium, the universal fluid.

Unless you are born of water and Spirit. In other words, unless you be born of water and fire...

Now, in order to help you to understand these two words, 'water' and 'fire', I must explain a little astrology to you. Of course, you all know the twelve signs of the zodiac: from the alchemical point of view, they correspond to the four elements: earth, water, air and fire, there being three signs for each element, and they are arranged on the circle of the zodiac in the order shown in Figure 1.

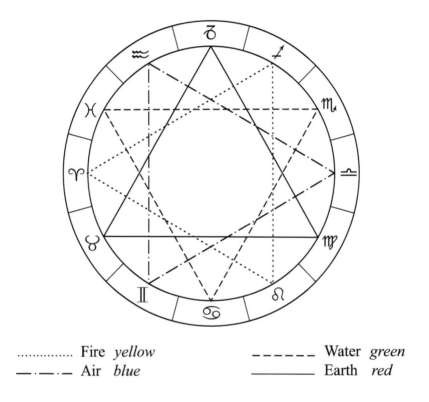

.... Fire *yellow*   — — — — — Water *green*
— · — · — Air *blue*   ————— Earth *red*

Figure 1

As you see, the signs belonging to each of the four elements are placed at the apex of four equilateral triangles. The triangle of earth is formed by the signs of Taurus ♉, Virgo ♍ and Capricorn ♑ ; the triangle of water is formed by the signs of Cancer ♋, Scorpio ♏ and Pisces ♓ ; the triangle of air is formed by the signs of Gemini ♊, Libra ♎ and Aquarius ♒, and the triangle of fire is formed by the signs of Aries ♈, Leo ♌ and Sagittarius ♐. I do not intend to talk about all the different possible combinations of these four triangles in every area of our lives. Today, we shall restrict ourselves to the two triangles of water and fire.

Each sign of the zodiac corresponds to a particular part of the human body (See Table), so that the triangles of water and fire give us the following (Figures 2 and 3):

Figure 2

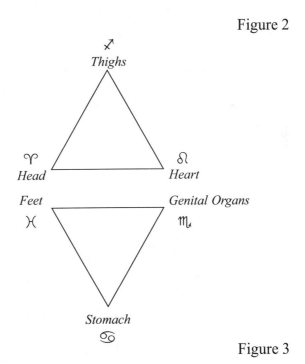

Figure 3

Table of correspondences between the zodiac and the human body.[4]

♈ Aries	Head	♎ Libra	Kidneys
♉ Taurus	Neck	♏ Scorpio	Genitals
♊ Gemini	Arms and lungs	♐ Sagittarius	Thighs
♋ Cancer	Chest and stomach	♑ Capricorn	Knees
♌ Leo	Heart	♒ Aquarius	Calves
♍ Virgo	Intestines	♓ Pisces	Feet

Each triangle also represents a cross-section of a triangular prism. You know what a prism is and you know that it decomposes white light into the spectrum of seven colours (See Figure 9). Nature has hidden tremendous secret meaning in this phenomenon. If the three sides of a prism are unequal, they will not distribute the colours in the same way as an equilateral triangle. Symbolically, these three sides of the prism represent the three principles in man: mind, heart and will or thought, feeling and action or any number of other phenomena or manifestations of life, such as: father, mother and child; acid, alkali and salt; light, heat and movement; love, wisdom and truth; length, breadth and height, etc., etc.

The phenomenon of the refraction of light by a prism is also based on three significant numbers: One, Three and Seven. The 1 represents the beam of white light that strikes the face of the prism; the 3 represents the prism itself with its three faces, and the 7 represents the spectrum of seven colours produced by the prism.

Let's take a look, now, at the different functions of our body, and you will see how they reproduce this phenomenon of the diffraction of light by a prism.[5] When we eat, for instance, the food represents the beam of white light (One) which passes through the prism, the stomach (Three), and produces the Seven, that is to say, the seven colours, the seven forces distributed throughout the body. In the phenomenon of breathing, we find the same thing: the air we inhale is the 1, the lungs represent the 3 and, here too, the 7 is represented by the seven forces distributed throughout the body.

But we can also study the prism from another point of view: if we say that the three sides of the prism correspond to the mind (thought), the heart (feeling) and the will (action), then an equilateral triangle is the symbol of a human being whose mind, heart and will are evenly developed (See Figure 4), of someone who is perfectly balanced, someone who is intelligent and, at the same time, both kind and capable of acting in accordance with his thoughts and feelings. Everything in him is harmonious. But, of course, as such people are few and far between, we can say that the equilateral triangle represents the Initiate, the Sage, the great Master.

Figure 4

Most men are irregular triangles, their sides are unequal. Some have a more highly developed will (Figure 5), which means that they are content to carry out other people's ideas. Others, on the

Figure 5   Figure 6

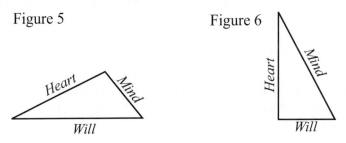

contrary, have developed their heart and mind to a far greater degree than their will (Figure 6), which means that they are capable of deep thought and careful analysis and, also, that they have deep feelings, but, when it comes to action, to putting their ideas into effect, they would rather let others act for them.

The triangle shown in Figure 7 symbolizes someone who is intelligent, active and energetic, but selfish and unkind, incapable of love or pity because his heart, his capacity for feeling, is underdeveloped. Whereas the triangle shown in Figure 8 represents someone whose heart and will are more developed than his intelligence: he will be very kind and generous and always ready to make sacrifices, but he will be a blunderer and an easy prey for others.

Figure 7   Figure 8

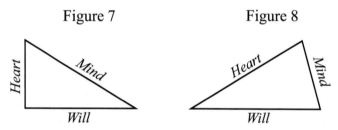

Obviously, there are so many possible combinations and variations that I cannot talk about them all; I can give you no more than a general outline. The essential thing to understand is that we must all make every effort to become equilateral prisms.

When the apex of a prism is at the top (Figure 9), the red is at the top of the band of colours and the violet at the bottom. If the apex points down, the order is reversed: the violet is above and the red below.

It is really marvellous to see how the colours of the spectrum are distributed in the human body: red is associated with the sexual organs; orange with the spleen; green with the stomach; blue with the lungs, and yellow, violet and indigo with the head. Each organ can be healed by its corresponding colour.

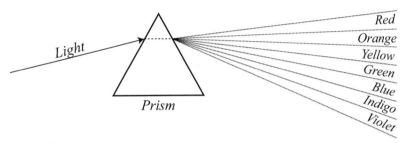

Figure 9

And now I want you to look at this figure (Figure 10):

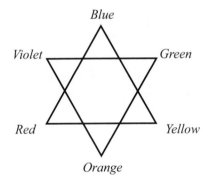

Figure 10

Let's begin with red: the mixture of yellow and red, which we see at the two lower angles of the same triangle, gives orange, which is the colour that lies between them, at the apex of the other triangle. Similarly, if we mix yellow and blue, we get green, whereas blue and red produce violet. But if we mix colours that are diametrically opposite, such as red and green, blue and orange or yellow and violet, the result is a very ugly colour. We must not mix these colours, therefore. This question of the affinity or incompatibility of colours conceals many truths. If we are ignorant of the laws which determine the predominant colour of each human being, we shall always be liable to do something that could have tragic consequences. These laws can also throw light on the consequences that we can expect from mixing certain thoughts and feelings, or even certain virtues and weaknesses. But this is a veritable spiritual alchemy and I do not intend to expand on it today. We shall have the opportunity to talk about it another time.

What I want to do is to explain to you, as simply as possible, the great truths on which man can base his existence and thanks to which he can improve his life and his relations with nature and the beings of the divine world. And I have promised myself to explain things in very clear, simple language, illustrated with plenty of examples and comparisons, even though I know that this may mean that I shall not be taken seriously: I shall be seen as a lecturer who regales his listeners with childish ideas and stories and never quotes any of the recognized authorities.

Take a sheet of red paper and a sheet of green, and put them side by side: the green will seem greener and the red will seem redder. When these two colours are side by side, they exalt each other but, as I have said, if you mix them you get a dirty, muddy colour. And the same is true of people.

Here is another experiment you can do: stare at a piece of red paper for a few seconds and then abruptly switch your gaze to something white: it will appear green. If you stare at something orange, you will see blue and if you stare at blue, you will see orange. Why? There are some very interesting laws involved here and these laws are reflected in our psychic life. Suppose you are meditating on something and, all of a sudden, a quite different idea crops up in your mind... This kind of phenomenon reveals the relationship between the red and green or the violet and yellow within you. Each virtue in man is related to another virtue, each quality to another quality, each movement to another movement, just as colours relate to each other. Also, each weakness is connected to another weakness. This means that a person need only stimulate one of his virtues or one of his failings and the corresponding virtue or failing will also be aroused. It is sometimes enough to trigger one passion in order to awaken another.

In fact, an even more intriguing phenomenon can be observed: if you make an effort to cultivate a particular virtue, the corresponding vice will sometimes make its appearance. The opposite can also be true at times: certain faults or failings can awaken a quality or virtue. These things should help us to understand how someone who has prayed regularly for years, who has always been a model of generosity and virtue, can suddenly fall a prey to a violent passion and indulge in all kinds of vices and excesses. How can someone who has always relied on heaven suddenly find his soul invaded by the forces of hell? On the other hand, we sometimes see just the reverse: people who have committed crimes and indulged in every form of vice become saints and models of kindness, purity and self-sacrifice.

We wish for purity but we often harbour impurity. We wish for wisdom but we often take pleasure in reading nonsense. Why do the Gospels say that matter is opposed to the spirit? Have you ever noticed how the branches of trees are linked to their roots? When the branches grow longer and thicker the roots, too, become stronger and go deeper into the ground. If a person does not know how the world above is linked to the world below, he will often be astonished by the results he obtains. But we shall come back to this question another time.

I have already told you that red is related to the genital organs and green to the stomach and liver. If the red in us is impure, it will cause the green in us to be impure also, which means that our stomach and liver will be unhealthy and fail to eliminate poisons from our system. All the colours are interrelated. He who follows the path of wisdom (yellow) is necessarily led to adore (violet) the Creator of the universe, the Lord of infinite wisdom.

violet corresponds to adoration and is the most spiritual of all the colours. Conversely, he who adores the Lord, who continually seeks him and makes the effort to be constantly in communion with him, will see that yellow begins to make its appearance; in other words, he begins to be wise.

What mysteries are still hidden in light! In the beginning was light...[6] To know light is to know all!

I have already told you that for alchemists and astrologers nature is composed of four fundamental elements: fire, air, water and earth, and if you observe life, you will see that water and fire are at the origin of almost every phenomenon on the face of the earth. Let's look at the following figure (Figure 11):

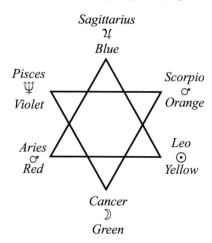

Figure 11

This figure represents the combination of the two triangles of fire and water. Any of you who have studied astrology will understand the profound significance of this symbol. The triangle of fire contains the three colours, red, yellow and blue. The red corresponds to Aries, the yellow to Leo and the blue to Sagittarius. These correspondences are in accordance with the nature of the signs and their ruling planets. Aries is ruled by Mars, the red planet, which is active, energetic and combative;

Leo is ruled by the Sun, and Sagittarius is ruled by Jupiter, the planet of religion and of a soaring spirituality.

The triangle of water includes the signs of Cancer, Scorpio and Pisces. Green corresponds to Cancer, orange to Scorpio and violet to Pisces. Cancer is the house of the Moon which governs a person's sensitivity and imagination. Like Aries, Scorpio is also the house of Mars, a house of independence, aggressiveness and pride. Pisces is the house of Neptune, a mystical house on the borderline between the two worlds.

Jesus said, *'No one can enter the kingdom of God without being born of water and Spirit'*. We interpret these words as follows: water corresponds to the heart, to love, to the passive, feminine principle. Fire corresponds to the spirit, to wisdom, to the active, masculine principle. We must be born, therefore, of these two principles, love and wisdom, in order to enter into the kingdom of God. These two principles, love and wisdom, give birth to truth. Do you know someone who claims to possess the truth? Ask if he possesses both love and wisdom. Ask him, 'Is your heart big enough to embrace the whole world? No? Does your mind understand all the laws of nature? No? Then you do not possess truth.' Truth is water and fire, love and wisdom, father and mother. And this is why men are, by nature, linked to wisdom and women to love.[7]

When our intellect becomes like the sun and our heart like water gushing from a spring, we shall be born for the second time. Astrology casts a horoscope only for the moment of a child's physical birth, of his first breath, but that is not enough. It is not possible to know someone's character or destiny on the basis of the moment of physical birth alone; you must also take into account the moment of conception as well as that of the second birth, which corresponds to the moment when consciousness becomes superconsciousness, to the moment when a person is illuminated and born anew in the other world. The most favourable moment for birth on earth can be calculated from the movements of the stars in the heavens, but it is not necessary to know anything about astrology in order to be born anew. It is enough to be rich in virtue and to live according to the laws of love, wisdom and purity, in order to be born again, to enter into the new life. Yes, because this new life is not a question of theoretical knowledge, it is a state of consciousness, a totality of thoughts, feelings and acts, a life lived for the benefit of others as well as for one's own benefit. On the other hand, of course, the esoteric sciences can be helpful if we study them in order to facilitate our evolution and arrive at a deeper understanding of the greatest mysteries.

It is a good practice, therefore, to study alchemy,[8] astrology,[9] magic[10] and the Cabbalah,[11] but if you want to understand them fully, you must begin by studying them in man. We cannot understand alchemy if we don't begin by studying true alchemy: human nutrition. We shall never really understand astrology if we do not study the human respiratory and circulatory systems, because the heart is the sun which illuminates the other planets, the organs, with its rays. The Cabbalah, on the other hand, with all the sephiroth and the angelic hierarchies, is contained in our heads, whereas magic is contained in our gestures: without realizing it, man makes magic – very often, black magic – with every gesture, grimace, look or word... with his whole behaviour.

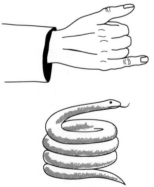

Figure 12

The exercises I am going to demonstrate to you are magical gestures, works of white magic. Every magus possesses a wand; you are familiar with the caduceus of Hermes which is a wand around which are twined two snakes. Hermes is the planet Mercury which rules in Gemini. The constellation of Gemini corresponds to our arms; in fact, you may have already noticed that the hands represent a snake (See Figure 12).

Someone who understands the two essential currents in nature can use his hands exactly as though they were a magic wand.

The exercises I am about to show you are based on very important laws. If you carry them out consciously and attentively you will obtain marvellous results for your health and every aspect of your personal equilibrium. There are many different currents in the universe, but the most important are the upward current which rises from the centre of the earth to the centre of the sun, and the downward current which flows in the opposite direction. The first exercise is related to the downward current and is intended to draw it into us and cause it to circulate perfectly within us. The second exercise is related to the upward current.

These two currents, ascending and descending, meet in our physical bodies on the level of the solar plexus which has the function of blending and distributing them correctly throughout our organism. This is very important, for if the two currents are incorrectly blended or unevenly distributed, they can cause our health to deteriorate very rapidly. It is important, therefore, to pay attention to the harmonious circulation of these two currents within us; this is the purpose of the exercises I shall now do in front of you.[12]

When I was in Bulgaria, I lived with a friend in the town of Ternovo, in a little house surrounded by trees and vines. It was in Ternovo that the Brotherhood gathered each year for a convention at which the Master was present. What I want to tell you is very interesting from both a spiritual and a scientific point of view. One day a magpie made a hole in the shutter of one of my windows and, not long after, a swarm of bees settled in the space between the shutter and the window pane and began to prepare the combs in which to store their honey. I was delighted to be able to watch them from my room and see exactly how they worked, and I saw some extraordinary things which were very rare from a scientific point of view. Many students of bees have built glass hives in the hope of watching bees at work, but they often hide themselves from the eyes of men by coating the glass partitions with some opaque matter. Here, however, they did not hide from me or from the many friends who came to visit us; it was as though we were living in a hive. The whole room was filled with the most marvellous intoxicating scent. It was so intoxicating, in fact, that it sometimes became almost unbearable and I found that it caused me to leave my physical body and live in the invisible world.

Watching the bees at work, I came to understand how pure they were and how highly evolved and, also, what a magnificent example they gave of a superior form of society. I cannot explain all that I learned from them, but what I can tell you is that bees are true disciples of the White Brotherhood, true symbols of beings who work hard and make honey, that extraordinary, delicious nourishment taken from flowers. The bees left a perfect image in my mind of how to make honey in life.

Bees did not come from this planet; no other insect can be compared to them. They came from the planet Venus especially for the benefit of initiates, ascetics and hermits, and of all those who spend their lives thinking of mankind, of God and of heaven. There is not very much food in the places where hermits and sages live and while they spend their time thinking about God, God also thinks of them, that is why he sent them the bees: to prepare this special kind of food for them. We are told that when the Earth saw this, it was jealous and tried to produce insects that would resemble the bees... and all it managed to produce was wasps! It was never able to find out how bees made honey, so wasps can do no more than build wax combs (but perhaps that is

Omraam Mikhaël Aïvanhov (1937)

only a fairy tale)! Wasps symbolize selfish, unworthy disciples
who are capable of eating honey but do not know how to make it,
who serve themselves before serving God. This is why nature's
secrets are hidden from them.

What is a bee's sting for? Perhaps you think its only purpose
is to allow the bee to defend itself against men or other insects
by stinging them? No, the principal function of a bee's sting is
not that of self-defence (in fact, it dies when it stings someone).
A bee's sting is used in making honey; it secretes a special
substance which is mixed with the honey in order to preserve it.
When honey does not contain this substance it is unfit for human
consumption.

I must tell you, also, that bees are so sensitive that they can
distinguish an evil, unjust, thieving man from one who is just,
kind and honest. They refuse to swarm anywhere near someone
who is unjust or a liar; they immediately go somewhere else.
Also, bees loathe disharmony and chaotic vibrations such as
fear, for example. And they hate garlic. If someone who has
been eating garlic gets anywhere near them they attack him
immediately! Now you understand why your stomach rebels if
you eat honey and garlic at the same meal!

Bees represent the sixth race of man, the race of the future,
the new culture. They love symmetry; haven't you already seen
the symmetry of the hexagonal cells they build? Also, they have
a detailed scientific knowledge of the colours and properties of
flowers. Bees are symbols of those who have been born anew.

He who has been born for the second time is like a living
fountain of pure water which gives birth to a new and thriving
civilization. His religion is the true religion of divine love and
wisdom. For him, the only true temple of God is the universe, the
sun is high priest in this temple and the stars are its votive lights.
He who has been born a second time is one who has opened
his secret, innermost channels so that they may be filled with
love and wisdom. He is the perfect prism that distributes the
seven beneficial forces throughout his own being and projects

them outwards for the benefit of all around him. He knows how to use the power of fire over water. He studies true alchemy, true astrology and the true Cabbalah which he finds, first and foremost, in himself. He is aware of his every gesture or movement, whether of his face or of his body. He watches over every word he utters.

He who has been born a second time resembles the bees: instead of devouring the leaves of plants, he hovers among the flowers, gathering from them the most delicious food that nature has to offer: their nectar. He who has been born again is capable of making honey.

My way of teaching you is not that of a master, for you are sons and daughters of God, and this means that all science and all knowledge are already in your possession. But by talking together of these things, we bring to mind all that we already knew, long, long ago, when we first came from the bosom of the Eternal Lord. This is what we shall try to do when we are together.

I hope that, one day, you too will visit the seven lakes of Rila, where we spend our summers out in the fresh air under the sun's rays, breathing freely, singing and rejoicing and thanking God for all his blessings, and where the crystal purity of the water flowing from the spring fills our hearts with the desire to resemble it.

Paris, 29 January 1938

Notes

1. See *The Yoga of Nutrition,* Izvor Coll. n° 204, chap. 7: 'Fasting: II – Another Form of Nutrition'.
2. See *The Living Book of Nature,* Izvor Coll. n° 216, chap. 3: 'Spring Water or Stagnant Water'.
3. See *The Mysteries of Fire and Water,* Izvor Coll. n° 232, chap. 4: 'Civilization, a Product of Water'.

4. See *Angels and other Mysteries of The Tree of Life,* Izvor Coll. n° 236, chap. 11: 'The Body of Adam Kadmon'.
5. See *The Splendour of Tiphareth – The Yoga of the Sun,* Complete Works, vol. 10, chap. 12: 'The Prism, Symbol of Man'.
6. See *Light is a Living Spirit,* Izvor Coll. n° 212, chap. 1: 'Light: Essence of Creation'.
7. See *Truth: Fruit of Wisdom and Love,* Izvor Coll. n° 234, chap. 2: 'Truth, the Child of Wisdom and Love', and *The Mysteries of Fire and Water,* Izvor Coll. n° 232, chap. 1: 'The Two Principles of Creation, Water and Fire'.
8. See *The Philosopher's Stone – in the Gospels and in Alchemy,* Izvor Coll. n° 241.
9. See *The Zodiac, Key to Man and to the Universe,* Izvor Coll. n° 220.
10. See *The Book of Divine Magic,* Izvor Coll. n° 226.
11. See *The Fruits of The Tree of Life – The Cabbalistic Tradition,* Complete Works, vol. 32, and *Angels and other Mysteries of The Tree of Life,* Izvor Coll. n° 236.
12. See *A New Earth – Methods, exercises, formulas, prayers,* Complete Works, vol. 13, Appendix: 'Description of physical exercises'.

Chapter Two

'ASK, AND IT WILL BE GIVEN TO YOU;
SEARCH, AND YOU WILL FIND;
KNOCK, AND THE DOOR WILL BE OPENED FOR YOU.'

This evening, I want to talk to you, again, about colours, for there are still a great many interesting things to be said on the subject. But, before I do that, I would like to take you on an expedition to breathe the pure air up in the mountains of Rila.

Our first port of call will be the summer camp of the Brotherhood. The brothers' and sisters' tents are pitched on the slopes rising from the edge of a lake of clear, limpid water, dotted with water anemones. From the level stretch of ground at the heart of the camp, we can look down at another plateau with another sleepy little lake. It has taken us seven hours to get up here; seven hours of sometimes rugged climbing through pastures and forests of fir trees, and now we are at an altitude of 2,300 metres and the whole panorama of the Bulgarian chain of mountains is laid out before us. But let me take you beyond the lake, beyond the rows of tents surrounding it, up towards the majestic, naked peaks above. As we climb, you will discover, one after another, five more lakes whose transparent waters reflect mountains and sky. The shape of these lakes is quite unusual: one of them looks like a heart, another like a stomach, a third like a kidney. The resemblance is so striking, in fact, that that is what they are now called. The highest of them is 'The Head'. It is also the smallest, and is linked to a larger lake, on almost the same level, by a sort of corridor. Several of the other lakes can be seen from here.

But we must not let the charm of the mountain flowers or the beauty of the landscape entice us to linger here; we still have a long climb ahead, for Musala Peak is 3000 metres high, the highest point of the Balkan mountains. Up here, the air is marvellously serene and translucid and the light that enfolds us so softly produces an extraordinary sensation of freedom and lightness.

And now, let's all sit down and, in the pure atmosphere of these mountain heights, interpret some of the familiar phenomena of our daily lives and see how they correspond to the realities of other dimensions.

You all know, for example, that our bodies are subject to the pressure of the atmosphere. This pressure is so great, in fact, that we should be completely flattened by it if it were not counteracted by our own, inner pressure. When we climb a mountain, the inner pressure is stronger than the atmospheric pressure; that is what gives us this sensation of lightness; in fact, if we went much higher, the inner pressure would be so great that our ears or even our skin might start to bleed. On the other hand, if we were to go down very far under the earth, the outer pressure would become more and more oppressive and stifling.

The same phenomena can be found in the spiritual life. Our consciousness can rise or it can descend. When it rises, the atmospheric pressure (which represents all those events and circumstances that confuse and torment us in life) weighs on us less and less heavily because the inner pressure becomes relatively stronger. If, on the contrary, our consciousness sinks down into the depths of matter, the slightest little problem seems to weigh on us like a mountain. Obviously, therefore, we must use our thoughts to carry us to greater heights so that we may live on the highest peaks of the spiritual mountains.

Atmospheric pressure symbolizes external circumstances, the material world, and the inner pressure of our bodies symbolizes the life principle, the spirit, which is perpetually struggling to manifest itself outwardly. There are two schools of thought in the world, which express these two tendencies: one which teaches that it is the external, material things that are essential in life, that everything depends on them, and another which teaches, on the contrary, that the spirit manifests itself through everything that exists and that it has the power to change material conditions.

When you feel crushed and born down by the weight of matter and external conditions, it means that your consciousness is dwelling on too low a level, and the atmospheric pressure has increased. And when you feel free and full of joy and strength, it means just the opposite: it means that you are up in the high mountains. He who has faith in the power of the spirit will see a gradual improvement in his circumstances. But he who believes that matter must inevitably extinguish the spirit will be the victim of his own point of view; he is ensuring the worst possible conditions for himself. The fact is, therefore, that both philosophies are true, but it depends on your point of view.

Let's look at the kinds of knowledge that we receive every day: very often they are purely theoretical. There was once a bishop, in Bulgaria, who was renowned for his marvellous sermons about charity. He used to say: 'If you have two shirts, you must not hesitate to give away one of them!' and there was such a world of pathos in his expression and his voice trembled with such emotion, that all those who heard him wept! One day, the bishop's wife was in church and was deeply moved by her husband's words. She knew that he possessed two shirts, so the first thing she did when she got home was to take his second shirt from the cupboard and give it to a beggar. Later, the bishop came home and wanted to change his shirt; not finding it in his cupboard, he called his wife and asked her where it was, and she, poor thing, confessed what she had done. At this, the bishop flew into a rage, but his wife said, 'But it was you yourself who said that if someone had two shirts he should not hesitate to give one of them away!' 'Stupid woman,' shouted her husband, 'I said that for others, not for us!'

And now, let me tell you another little story. There was once a very brilliant scholar who had hired a man to take him out to sea in his rowing boat. He asked the boatman, 'My good man, do you know anything about astronomy?' 'No.' replied the boatman. 'What a pity,' said the scholar; 'You are missing so much; a quarter of your life is wasted. But, perhaps you know something about physics?' 'Not a thing, Your excellency!' said the boatman. 'Oh, my poor man, two quarters of your life are lost!' lamented the scholar; 'But perhaps you know a lot of chemistry?' 'What's that?' said the boatman; 'Never heard of it!' 'What ignorance,' lamented the scholar; 'Three quarters of your life gone to waste!' The little boat went farther and farther out to sea and, before long, a violent storm blew up and the waves threatened to engulf them. 'Your honour,' cried the boatman; 'Do you know how to swim?' 'No, I don't.' replied the scholar. 'Well, sir,' exclaimed the boatman; 'That's four quarters of your life gone to waste!'

You see? There are some kinds of knowledge which are perfectly useless. They are nothing more than decorations. Oh, to be sure, they can be used to earn money, but if a storm comes along you will soon see if they can help you to swim! Life is an ocean, as you very well know, and in that ocean there are some kinds of knowledge which are much more useful than others: the knowledge that can help a man to live. What direction to give to our life; which high ideal to choose; how to transform the thoughts and feelings that disturb us; how to interpret the events taking place around us; how to ascertain our relations with the macrocosm; how to eat, sleep, wash and breathe... how to love: these are the things we need to know.

The essence of life is to be in harmony with the higher world, the divine world.

Jesus said, *'Ask, and it will be given to you; search, and you will find; knock, and the door will be opened for you.'* These words refer to prayer, and it is very important to know how to pray. Often, though, not only do people not know how to pray, but they feel a certain repugnance towards prayer, and despise those who pray. Nowadays, prayer is not a very fashionable thing to do! People consider themselves educated and enlightened and think that it is absurd for an educated man to pray to God!

'Ask, and it will be given to you; search, and you will find; knock, and the door will be opened for you.' One can understand these words only if one understands that, in man, there is the trinity of intellect, heart and will. *'Ask, and it will be given to you...'* But what should you ask for? And what or who is it in man that asks? And who seeks? Who knocks? It is the heart that asks, the intellect that seeks, and the will that knocks. The heart asks... Yes, and what does it ask for? Not for knowledge, light or wisdom; it asks for warmth, tenderness and love. And the intellect, the mind, does not ask: it seeks. But the mind seeks neither warmth nor love, for it cannot function too well when it is warm, it is inclined to go to sleep! What the intellect seeks is methods, light. And it is the will that knocks; it knocks because it is in prison and needs space and freedom in order to create.

So here we have yet another application of the symbolism of this triangle (Figure 13).

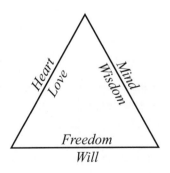

Figure 13

The heart's ideal is divine love; the mind's ideal is divine wisdom, and the ideal of the will is divine power. Freedom can only be won through truth which is the fusion of love and wisdom. Jesus said, *'The truth will make you free'*.

If you want to understand this question in greater depth, let me say that love, wisdom and freedom are no other than the elixir of everlasting life, the philosophers' stone and the magic wand sought by all the sages. Yes, it is love that bestows the elixir of everlasting life. Men have always sought it in vain because they have sought it without love, and without love it cannot be found. Only love can give true life, immortal life. Whereas he who seeks, seeks wisdom and light; one does not look for something in the dark, but in the light of day. This is why the word 'seek' is always linked to light and wisdom. He who seeks light will find the philosophers' stone, the Mercury of the sages, the key that can unlock all the secrets of nature and enable him to understand the bonds that hold things together. And the door will be opened to those who possess integrity and rectitude of will; they will receive the gift of freedom, the magic wand.

The elixir of everlasting life is divine love.

The philosophers' stone is divine wisdom.

The true magic wand is the truth which bestows absolute freedom.

When Jesus said, *'Ask, and it will be given to you; search, and you will find; knock, and the door will be opened for you'*, he implied, therefore, that prayer was efficacious only when the three principles of intellect, heart and will were involved. When your heart, mind and will pray with one voice, then, yes: your prayer will be heard, because your whole being is one with the invisible world. If your prayers are not answered, you must not conclude that God does not exist but that you have been praying mechanically, without the participation of your heart or will.[1]

Let me tell you two stories that will teach you more than any number of speeches about prayer. Among the monks of a certain monastery, there was one who was a very simple, ignorant man. He spent his days sweeping the floor and washing the dishes and, while he did this, he would pray with all his heart: 'Lord God, as I wash these dishes, wash my soul... As I clean this floor, cleanse my heart of all impurities.' After years and years of praying in this way, he had become so pure and holy and full of light, that bishops and cardinals would come and consult him, for the Holy Spirit was with him.

And now for the second story: one day a bishop took a little boat and went for a row on a lake up in the mountains. When he reached the other side of the lake, he saw a shepherd tending his sheep and was struck by his expression, for it revealed such peace and joy. The bishop got into conversation with him and, after a while, he asked him if he believed in God and how he prayed. The shepherd, who was honoured and overjoyed by the bishop's question, replied, 'Oh, that's simple: when I want to thank God I put my crook down on the ground and skip over it, back and forth, back and forth, like this!' The bishop was horrified. 'That's ridiculous!' said he; 'That's not the way to pray. I'll show you...' Then he explained to the shepherd how he should get down on his knees and what words he should use to express his gratitude to God. The shepherd listened with great humility and was very glad to learn how to pray better. Then the bishop left him, went back to his boat and pushed out towards the far side. All of sudden, when he had already gone quite a long way, what did he see but the shepherd, running towards him, calling out, 'Reverend father, tell me the words of the prayer, again. I've forgotten them.' Amazed to see that poor man walking on the water, the bishop replied, 'Oh, my son, pray in whatever way you like; you know much more about it than I do!'

It sometimes happens that we meet unsophisticated people who know nothing about philosophy or science but who are truly alive. Why didn't Christ live among the learned? Don't misunderstand me, I have nothing against people who are learned; I, too, want to learn as much as possible. But I want you to understand that we often forget the most important thing in life, which is gratitude to God. On the one hand, we have a lot of useless knowledge and, on the other, we think that the world is badly organized, so we give God the benefit of our advice and try to improve his way of doing things by substituting our own... Because, of course, we know so much better!

You will tell me that there is nothing more important than science. But there is: we must learn to be grateful to God. To give thanks to the Lord every day and be pleased with what he gives you is to possess the secret magic capable of transforming your whole life. When you are grateful, light and love increase within you and your actions are enhanced. You look at the world with other eyes and, one day, you will find that men open their hearts to you because you radiate light and joy. Those who meet you will feel drawn to you and God will touch their hearts and help you through them. They will say, 'What a wonderful person he is! I'd like to do something to help him.'

However many doors you knock on, if heaven's banks are shut, no one will give you anything because, in the final analysis, it is not human beings who give. If the banks on high are closed to you, therefore, no one will listen to you on earth, either: heaven will prevent men from giving you anything.

When I tell you that you are extremely wealthy, you don't believe me. But let me prove to you that, although you don't know it, you are all billionaires! Suppose I said, 'You're always complaining that you are poor. Very well, I'll give you ten million in exchange for your hands!' You would refuse to give them to me, wouldn't you? 'All right, what about a hundred million for your eyes?' Again you would refuse. And if I tried to buy your tongue or your nose for fabulous sums of money, you would still refuse... in other words you are billionaires! If a big landowner who has great estates and mansions is short of cash, that does not mean to say that he is poor! You think that you are poor because your wealth is not in the form of gold or banknotes, but the truth is that that kind of money is of no real use to you.

You have no idea about what is really valuable and what is not. You often give away your peace for next to nothing, and then, when you want to communicate with the Lord, your inner landscape has lost the serenity conducive to this communication. Often enough, you give away your minds, too. But there is a hierarchy of values in nature and you must learn, henceforth, to distinguish between what is really important and what is less so.

Let's get back to the image of the prism. If the prism points downwards, the spectrum of colours ranges from violet, at the top, to red, below (Figure 14).

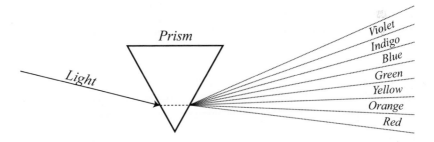

Figure 14

Colours can teach us how to get into touch with the higher worlds and all the White Brotherhoods on earth. Red is the

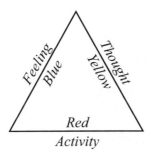

colour with the lowest frequency of vibrations; it is related to man's vital functions. In the triangle of heart, mind and will that we talked about last time, red represents the will. Yellow represents intelligence, wisdom, the faculty of thought, and blue represents religious sentiments, gentleness, music, the heart.

All colours relate to specific areas of the brain which has centres that act as antennae, each one of which picks up a particular range of waves. If you have a series of tuning forks, each one of which is tuned to a different pitch, when you cause one of them to vibrate, the others remain silent. But if, among your tuning forks, there are two which are tuned to the same frequency, when you make one of them vibrate, the other will begin to resonate in harmony with it. Our brain is constructed according to the laws of nature. Each of its centres is like a tuning fork tuned to resonate in response to certain waves. When the vibrations of red, for instance, reach the brain, only the centres at the back of the skull resonate. Red excites sexual love (centre situated at the back of the head) and the centres above and behind the ears, which correspond to destruction and cruelty. You can see for yourselves that the heads of the more ferocious animals are very broad on the level of the ears. A skull that is very broad at this level, therefore, denotes someone who is cruel and destructive and who would certainly be a criminal unless his spiritual centres are also so well developed that they prevent his criminal tendencies from manifesting themselves.

The vibrations of yellow reach and penetrate all our organs, but the only tuning forks that respond to them are the centres situated in the middle and upper part of the forehead. If we immerse ourselves in yellow, it helps to develop our scientific and philosophical faculties. If we immerse ourselves in the vibrations of blue, on the other hand, they excite the centres of spirituality situated on the top of the head.

All kinds of currents flow through nature; some of them have the effect of vivifying us while others, on the contrary, tend to have a disintegrating effect. We can use the properties of these currents to descend to hell or to raise ourselves to the highest summits. If we want to be in harmony with the beneficial currents in the universe, we must entertain only elevated thoughts and pure, spiritual feelings.

Last Saturday, I told you that the alchemy of life was to be found in the stomach, that astrology was to be found in the functions of respiration and circulation, that the brain was linked to the Cabbalah and the arms to magic. In what way? When we eat we are building our own edifice, the temple of the spirit.[2] If the matter that we absorb and use as building materials for our temple is not pure, we cannot vibrate in harmony with the right kind of currents. If we eat meat, for instance, the cells of the dead animals become an integral part of our own body and, as they are unfriendly and hostile to us, when we want to do something noble, they oppose our wishes and refuse to cooperate. Also, when we eat meat, we absorb elements that belong to the animal kingdom such as fear, cruelty and so on, and this means that it will be very difficult for us to develop our higher Self, because the animal cells will refuse to obey us. They have their own will which opposes ours. You will say, 'Oh, but meat is so delicious!' Perhaps, but if you asked microbes for their opinion, they would tell you that human flesh was delicious, too! What I am telling you, today, is addressed to those who want to evolve; the others can behave as they please, but, in the long run, they will pay dearly for their mistakes.

We must eat pure food, but we must also allow only pure feelings and pure thoughts to enter us. This is the best way to rise to a higher level, to climb all the way up the mountain until we reach the summit.

If you look at the astrological symbol for the sun ⊙, you will see that it represents the summit of a mountain, for this symbol is the geometrical projection of the tip and circular base of a cone (Figure 16).

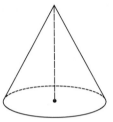

Figure 16

This symbol ⊙, is the symbol of the sun, and the sun is the centre of our planetary system. It also represents the eye, for our two eyes are also mountains: the right eye is the mountain of the sun and the left eye the mountain of the moon. But we shall come back to that another day.

And now I'm going to tell you an immortal story which, I am sure, you all know. Once upon a time there was a king who had a daughter. For some reason that I have forgotten, this girl had been asleep for a long time; she was shut up in a palace full of fabulous treasures and guarded by a dragon. Many princes attempted to rescue her but none succeeded. And then, one day, a prince who was braver, nobler and handsomer than any of the others succeeded where all others had failed: he defeated the dragon and rescued the princess and, climbing onto the back of the vanquished dragon, they flew away up into the air. What does this tale mean? The princess is our soul and the dragon represents our passions and vices. The prince who manages to rescue the princess is our spirit, and it rescues the soul thanks to wisdom (for the prince knew), thanks to love (he had an ardent love for the princess and it was his love that enabled him to overcome all the obstacles put before him) and thanks to the will, for will-power is the only true power. Love, wisdom and truth enable us to tame the passions within us, to transform them and, finally, to use them for our work in the world. And this means that, if we want to rescue our soul from the clutches of the dragon (the passions) we must ask, every day, for divine love, we must seek the methods of divine wisdom and we must never stop knocking to obtain freedom.

There is an absolute principle in nature by which that which is inferior is obliged to obey that which is superior; but if the superior deviates and falls into grave error, its inferiors rebel and destroy it. If the white race, for instance, continues to be concerned only with the satisfaction of its own selfish propensities, it will awaken the forces of evil that surround it (in fact, it is clear that this has already begun), and these forces will use whatever channels are available in order to manifest themselves. This awakening is not something that happens overnight; it is a process that advances slowly but inexorably, like a landslide or a flow of lava, but on a gigantic scale. The consequences will be such that, one day, the whole of Europe will be involved. Astrologers have always foretold this: if the white race does not pull itself together, the yellow and black races will arouse themselves from their state of subservience and obedience, and destroy it. In view of the way in which people in the West solve their problems, the results can only be disastrous. The intellect is not enough... Knowledge is not enough... It is time for another form of culture, a culture of love and brotherliness among men.

Between the higher and lower worlds are a series of barriers comparable to the barrier formed by the solar plexus, a kind of astral diaphragm which prevents inferior elements from reaching the higher levels.[3] When a person is pure, his solar plexus can defend his organism against invasion by inferior elements, but if he does not live by the rules of nature, he leaves himself open to invasion by forces from below. If Europeans continue to live lives of impurity and disorder, they will finally rupture the invisible barriers that protect them and unleash the negative forces into every area of life. There are no words to express what will happen. Only one thing can save Europe and that is a living bond of brotherly love between all men.

France is now my country and my love for it is sincere. And there is still a great deal that we can do for our country; it only depends on you and on all its citizens. We must prepare strong, powerful waves by imploring heaven's blessing on France and Europe and the whole of mankind.

Before concluding, I must come back briefly to one or two ideas.

Never allow your consciousness to descend to such depths that you no longer feel the power of the spirit within you, that you feel yourself stifled by material conditions. Climb to the spiritual heights where you can get a breath of pure air and a clear view of reality.

When you pray, make sure that your intellect, heart and will all participate in your prayer. Ask for the elixir of everlasting life which is divine love; seek the philosophers' stone which is divine wisdom, and knock with your will to obtain freedom through just, honest and truthful actions.

Among all the different kinds of knowledge available to you, choose those that can teach you to swim in the ocean of life. Be assured that the one and only force which can enable you to perform miracles in life is to be found, not in philosophical or theoretical knowledge, but in the simplicity of your life and in the manifestation of love, faith and hope.[4] This is why the shepherd, whose life was simple and sincere, was closer to the truth than the bishop whose head was packed with theoretical knowledge.

If we want to change our destiny we must cultivate sentiments of gratitude, because gratitude contains a magic power far stronger and more potent than all the talismans manufactured by men.

If we want to have control over our passions and instincts and for all our cells to obey our instructions, we need to eat pure, vegetarian food.[5]

Only a life of purity can protect us from invasion by inferior forces. Purity is the barrier that keeps us safe from every invasion of evil. Thanks to love, wisdom and truth, we, who are true princes, shall rescue our souls from the clutches of the dragon and fly away with them on the back of the conquered dragon, to visit the universe and contemplate its beauty and hear its celestial harmonies. Then we shall understand how glorious life is and how full of meaning.

> *'Ask, and it will be given to you;*
> *search, and you will find;*
> *knock, and the door will be opened for you.'*

Paris, 5 February 1938

Notes

1. See *La Prière,* Brochure n° 305.
2. See *Creation: Artistic and Spiritual,* Izvor Coll. n° 223, chap. 12: 'Building the Temple'.
3. See *Man's Subtle Bodies and Centres – the Aura, the Solar Plexus, the Chakras...,* Izvor Coll. n° 219, chap. 3: 'The Solar Plexus'.
4. See *The Faith That Moves Mountains,* Izvor Coll. n° 238, chap. 1: 'Faith, Hope and Love'.
5. See *The Yoga of Nutrition,* Izvor Coll. n° 204, chap. 4: 'Choosing Your Food', and chap. 5: 'Vegetarianism'.

Chapter Three

TRUTH IS HIDDEN IN THE EYES

This evening I propose to talk to you about colours, again, but the point of view will be different from that which I took in the last two lectures.

You are all familiar with the five-pointed star that we call the pentagramme. Our Master Peter Deunov has often said that the pentagramme symbolizes a man who has developed the five virtues to an equal degree of perfection: kindness, justice, love, wisdom and truth. Looking at it from another point of view, one can also say the pentagramme represents the five senses: touch, taste, smell, hearing and sight.[1] The five virtues can be set out on the pentagramme as shown in Figure 17.

Figure 17

The Master also gave us the following rule: 'Take kindness as the foundation of your life, justice as the yardstick, wisdom as a barrier, love as a delight and truth as light.'

If you reflect on these precepts for a moment, you cannot help but be struck by the truth of them.

Everything must be built on kindness. However much intelligence and beauty has gone into the construction of the edifice, if it is not upheld by kindness it will crumble.

Justice is a quality which enables us to measure things, to evaluate and distinguish them one from another.

Without love, life is insipid; even if someone possesses great wealth, intellectual learning and worldly renown, without love he will have no zest for life.

Wisdom is a barrier; thanks to wisdom we can defend the good qualities God has given us against erosion by negative forces and other enemies, both visible and invisible. If we are lacking in wisdom, wild animals will break in and trample the garden of our life.

Truth is the light that lights our path. Without it we shall always dwell in darkness, falsehood and error.

These five virtues are essential to the development of man but, unfortunately, very few people know that there is a link between these virtues and the human body. And yet, true science, as well as all success and all achievements in life, lies in the knowledge of this link. Kindness is related to the legs, justice to the arms and hands, love to the mouth, wisdom to the ears and truth to the eyes.

The five virtues are also represented by the five fingers of the hand, thanks to which we have the possibility of doing and creating.

Today, I shall talk to you about the eyes.

There is a great deal to be said about the eyes. As you know, there is a science known as iridology which studies the iris of the eye in the minutest detail and thanks to which all one's past and present illnesses can be discerned. All the organs of the body, including the eyes themselves, are represented in the iris in such detail that even the loss of a tooth can be detected. It is often said that the eyes are the mirror of the soul, and it is true. Wisdom, kindness and all the other hidden qualities of a man can be seen in his eyes.

The eye is represented diagrammatically as a circle with a dot in the centre ⊙. As you know, this is also the astrological symbol for the sun. For an astrologer, the right eye is related to the sun and the left to the moon, and if the sun and moon are poorly aspected in a person's horoscope, his eyes will suffer in some way, either by illness or by accident; it depends on the aspects of the planets and the houses in which they are placed.

Initiates have studied all the images of nature very closely, and have observed the signs inscribed on our hands and faces, on plants and stones and in the stars, and they have summed up some of their discoveries in the astrological signs. Today, therefore, I shall try to show you the profound meaning of this symbol of the eye, but I am going to have to ask you to be patient! When you see an artist in the street, in the process of painting a picture, you see lines and splashes of colour which seem to mean nothing. But if you stay and watch, little by little, you will see that the lines fit together, the colours harmonize and the whole picture becomes clearly recognizable. Well, I am here in the role of that artist and you have to be patient and, for the time being, agree simply to look at the different strokes of the brush as I lay them on the canvas before you.

From earliest antiquity, men have used images and symbols to express the most profound truths. If we want to interpret these images and symbols, however, we have to breathe the life of the spirit into them, for they represent the living realities of our inner life. They mean nothing if we study them only as external realities. In the old days, Masters gave their disciples symbolic figures (figures such as those that now make up the Tarot cards, for instance), which they had to vivify. In other words, they had to discover what they meant and how they applied to their own lives. So if we can find the underlying meaning of the shape of our mouth and tongue, of our ears, including the organ of Corti, and of our eyes, we shall be opening up a prodigious fund of knowledge.

The symbol of the eye is present everywhere, in every domain: in physiology, mathematics, astrology, botany, alchemy and in the mineral, vegetable, animal and human kingdoms, and we must try to discover it wherever it is. I have already said that it is used in astrology to represent the sun, but why is it shown with a dot in the centre? The circle is the symbol of the universe, of the Supreme Being, and the dot represents the manifestation of this Being. A circle without a dot in the centre represents the unmanifested Supreme Being, the Absolute; when it contains a central dot, it represents the Supreme Being in a state of manifestation.[2]

Looking at this symbol from another point of view, we can say that it represents a cell: the central dot is the nucleus; the space between the centre and the periphery is the protoplasm, and the circle represents the membrane. The masculine principle manifests itself by rectilinear radiations and the feminine principle by circular waves. Electricity travels in a straight line, whereas magnetism forms circular waves. The electrical currents which are present in such abundance at high altitudes in the mountains, move parallel to the ground, sweeping the soil and rocks clean by killing all vegetation. In the plains, by contrast, where magnetic currents manifest themselves, vegetation is abundant. We shall find the same laws at work in the human physiognomy: all the elongated, linear forms are modeled by electricity, and the rounded forms by magnetism. The masculine principle at work in nature creates straight, linear forms and the feminine principle creates curved, rounded forms. The symbol that represents the two principles at work in the universe is that of the sun manifesting itself both in the form of rays extending from a central point and in concentric circles spreading out from the centre to the periphery (Figure 18).

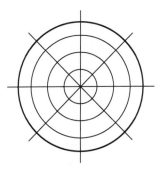

Figure 18

We find this figure in the cross-section of a tree trunk in which both the masculine and feminine principles are at work.

But, let's get back to the subject of the eye. You know that the pupil of your eye dilates in the dark, whereas it contracts in the light. The brighter the light, the smaller it gets. The dilation and contraction of the pupil follow a curved, circular movement. When the pupil is fully contracted, the eye is an exact replica of the symbol of the sun.

For the alchemist, this symbol ☉ is also the symbol for gold. Gold is a noble metal that never corrodes because it is a condensation of the sun's rays. In fact, this is why men have an instinctive love of gold, because of its connection with the sun. The sun's rays travel through space and penetrate into the depths of the earth where the nature spirits that dwell underground collect the solar forces they contain and use them to manufacture gold. Gold, therefore, is simply a condensation of solar energy. A person who has a lot of gold is rich and respected in the world, but it is not enough to possess gold outwardly; we also have to possess it inwardly, for it is that inner gold that enables us to withstand illness, suffering and discouragement.[3] For the time being, I shall say no more about this; I leave each one of you free to believe what I say or not, as you please.

From the geometrical point of view, this symbol ⊙ is the projection of a cone. I have already explained to you that each colour corresponds to a particular frequency and that the frequency becomes progressively higher as it moves up the scale from red to violet. The colours of the spectrum follow each other in an uninterrupted sequence; we cannot tell, for instance, exactly where orange ends and yellow begins. We can only say with certainty that here we see yellow and there we see orange, but it is impossible to find the exact line of demarcation. And this is true in a great many areas in which we can neither detect nor fix limits. Naturally, if you stand a good way off and look at things from outside, you can say: 'This is good and that is bad', but if you try to put your finger on the fine line that divides the two, you cannot do it; no one can. We can only say that that which is bad is the inferior aspect and that that which is good the superior, but the passage from one to the other is imperceptible. And with the body and the soul it is the same: you cannot tell exactly where the body ends and the soul begins. And how could anyone hope to determine the exact limits of the etheric, astral and mental bodies? Everyone agrees that they are different and distinct from each other, but no one can explain exactly how they are connected to each other nor how the transformational processes of the soul correspond to those of the body.

The same pattern repeats itself in every domain of life: everything moves imperceptibly upwards, and this is something we should be glad of, for it is this that enables us, too, to move up from one level to the next, all the way to the summit. Sometimes we feel that we are in paradise: we are full of gladness and confidence, and then, only a few hours later, we come tumbling down again and feel as though we were in hell: all is sorrow, pain and despair. Later, I shall talk to you about how to move up and down on this Jacob's ladder of vibrational frequencies.

The frequencies of luminous vibrations form a continuous spectrum ranging from the longest (red) to the shortest (violet)

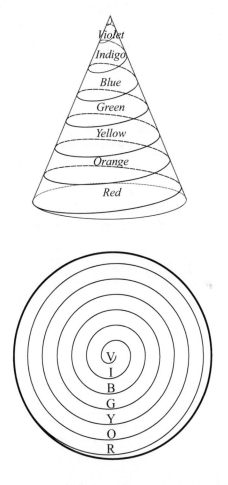

Figure 19

and, as light revolves symmetrically round the axis of its rectilinear propagation, the chain of this succession of vibrations forms a conical spiral (Figure 19).

The tip of the cone, which represents the centre of the circle, corresponds to the shortest wavelengths, that is, the highest frequencies. It is here, at this point, that true spiritual peace is to be found, for spiritual peace is not a static condition: it is a state of intense vibration and of the highest and most sublime form of activity. It is in this state of peace that the spirit manifests itself most perfectly. The cone is a symbol of the sun as well as that of a mountain and the initiates have hidden tremendous secrets in this symbol. Anyone who has scaled the slopes of a mountain, whether physical or spiritual, understands this symbol of the sun: from the summit he can see everything in all directions. From the symbolic point of view, it is the sun that is the summit, the culminating point of our system. All good comes to us from the sun. It is through the sun that God manifests himself and sends us his blessings.

The eyes are related to truth. Jesus said, *'If your eye is healthy, your whole body is full of light.'* Of course, Jesus was not talking about our physical eyes but about the spiritual eye, that which we call the third eye, the mystical eye that enables us to see the whole of reality.[4] The two physical eyes and the third eye form a triangle, a prism (Figure 20), thanks to which the currents that flow through us, as well as all our thoughts and feelings, strengthen our aura and enhance our sensitivity to the divine world.

At the moment, the only light that enters us is the light we receive through our physical eyes; our third eye is closed by inferior thoughts and feelings that prevent us from perceiving currents from above. The only ones we are capable of picking up – in fact, we cannot avoid doing so – are those from below.

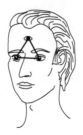

Figure 20

The third eye of an initiate is an antenna which puts him in touch with the divine world. We would do well to practise concentrating on our third eye every day; it is a very good exercise which makes it possible to attain an extraordinary degree of elevation from which we see things from a quite different point of view. Imagine two people who are examining a very large sphere: one of them is standing on the outside and one on the inside. The person outside the sphere says that it is convex, while the one who is inside contradicts him and says that it is concave: if they stick to their limited points of view, the argument can only become more and more acrimonious and they will never agree. These two people are science and religion: science looks at the universe from the outside and says that it is convex, whereas religion looks at it from the inside and says that it is concave. And then a third person comes along and says: 'You are both right and both wrong: the universe is neither concave nor convex, it is both at the same time!' Yes, he can say this because he sees things simultaneously from inside and from outside. The inner eye, intuition, sees both aspects at once; it is this intuition that we must cultivate in order to see both inwardly and outwardly at the same time.

The outer dimension is the domain of the intellect; the inner dimension is the domain of the heart, of feeling. When you look at things only from the intellectual point of view, you can classify and analyse them but you cannot feel them. Whereas, if you look at them from the point of view of your feelings, you may be touched and moved by them, but you will not know their external manifestations. Neither the subconscious nor self-consciousness can reveal the whole truth; only the super-conscious, cosmic consciousness, is capable of doing that. The subconscious draws energy and knowledge from the depths of creation, from the roots, the basic instincts of man; self-consciousness draws them from shapes and appearances. Only a third point of view which combines the two, can reveal the whole of reality. It is this third point of view which men must now cultivate. Everyone is more or less prejudiced in his opinions; no wonder, in these conditions, that people make so many mistakes. Depending on his personal tastes and inclinations, each one sees only one aspect of reality; no wonder they have such difficulty understanding each other and living harmoniously together!

I have mentioned the super-conscious, but it is, perhaps, a notion that is not quite clear to you, so let me explain it by means of a very simple example. Suppose you receive a blow on the head and fall down in a faint: you are in a state of unconsciousness. Thanks to the ministrations of your friends who try to reanimate you, you begin to move very slightly. You still cannot open your eyes or regain consciousness: you are in a state of subconsciousness. This is the state of someone who stirs in his sleep. But, before long, you open your eyes and, although you still do not remember what happened to you, you realize that you are lying on the ground surrounded by your friends: this is the state of consciousness. Then you gradually come round completely and remember what happened: you have reached the state of self-consciousness. Finally, you feel stronger, you get to your feet, smile at those kind friends who have been helping you and remember that you have a lot to look forward to, and a lot to be thankful for, so you feel happy and full of hope and gratitude to God: you have reached the state of superconsciousness.

Unconsciousness corresponds to the mineral kingdom, the subconscious corresponds to the vegetable kingdom, consciousness belongs to the animal kingdom, self-consciousness belongs to the domain of human beings and superconsciousness to the domain of the angels, which is also the domain of masters, initiates and supermen. The state of superconsciousness is a state in which we are capable of tuning in to the waves emitted by heaven and by initiates. There are certain mystical centres on this earth, in which initiates pray constantly for the illumination and happiness of mankind. Unfortunately, not many human beings receive and benefit from these waves, because they never do anything to develop their aura which is the best conductor, the perfect antenna, capable of picking them up. The aura is the cone, the mantle of seven colours through which we rise to the summit. The cone, therefore, is a symbol of spiritual elevation, of the ascension to the divine world; but if it points downwards, it becomes the symbol of the hell described by Dante. The more sinful a man is, the lower he sinks towards the bottom of the cone, that is to say: the more he suffers and the more closely he is restricted by his bonds. Those who reach the very bottom of the cone are totally restricted... But I don't like to talk about the inverted cone for, simply by thinking about it, we are led to experience the states that it represents.

And now I want to say a few words about the aura and how to develop and intensify it. Our higher Self is the central dot in the circle of our being.[5] It is the point of greatest harmony, a point of utter stillness and peace in the midst of a world of movement. This does not mean that this point of light is static or immobile; it seems immobile because it vibrates so rapidly that we cannot see the movement. In reality, peace is the most intense form of activity there is. Usually, you will agree, the word 'peace' conjures up the picture of a man eating and drinking, stretched out in the shade of a beautiful tree... No, that is not peace! Peace is the most intense form of work that exists: not aimless agitation, but intense movement. By consciously putting ourselves in touch, every day, with this point in our head or solar plexus, we attain a sense of inner peace; sorrow, anxiety and anguish no longer have the power to touch us.[6] Whereas, if we fail to make conscious contact with this point, neither we nor anyone else will be able to free us from torment, and we can expect no help from external remedies such as medication or drugs.

This is only a very brief explanation, but it should help you to understand that in studying the symbolism of the eye, we are studying the symbolism of the magic circle. You all know that when an initiate intends to perform a magic rite, he draws one or more concentric circles on the ground and steps into the centre where he will be protected. If he were to leave the protection of the circle too soon he would put himself in great danger. But we must look for this magic circle inside ourselves, not on the outside; everything has to be understood inwardly, not just outwardly. The best possible protection we can have is the circle of our own aura; it fills exactly the same function as the earth's atmosphere. If the earth were suddenly deprived of its atmosphere, the result would be a series of fearful cataclysms and we, like the planet earth, are surrounded by an atmosphere that protects us from the dangers of the outside world.

Let me give you an example. Suppose that you bump into a piece of furniture and bruise yourself: your skin turns black and blue. Later, if someone touches you on the bruise, you cry out from pain, whereas, if your skin were healthy, you would not feel anything at all. Well, the aura is exactly like our skin; it is our spiritual skin. This surprises you, perhaps; at first sight you see no connection between the aura and the skin. But let's take a quick look at the principal functions of the skin. First of all, it protects us from impurities and shocks from the environment; secondly, it is an organ of exchange between the body and that environment, and, finally, it is a sense organ that keeps us informed about heat and cold, changes of climate and so on. And our aura has exactly the same functions as the skin, but on another level. If it is powerful and bright, it protects us against accidents in the spiritual world, whereas, if it is flimsy or unhealthy, even hostile thoughts and feelings can injure us and cause considerable suffering.

I have often heard people say, for instance, 'When he looked at me like that, it was as though he'd stuck a knife into me!' If they had worked to develop their aura, they would not have been nearly so deeply affected. It is very important in life to be protected by a strong, healthy aura. I have known a lot of sick people whose illness was not caused by anything physical; it was due to the inadequacy of their aura. The second function of the aura is to ensure a continual exchange between the stars outside us and those within. If our aura is impure and sombre it will pick up only harmful currents because it will be incapable of picking up the good ones. It is often said that some planets are benefic and others malefic, but if that were true, how should we account for the fact that the same planet can have a good effect on some people and a bad one on others? It is simply that some receive only the ill effects of a planet because they are not capable of tuning in to its beneficial currents. The truth is that all the planets are benefic, but the effect they have on each individual depends on his aura. If his aura contains colours and layers that act as a barrier to positive influences, the currents carrying the virtues of that planet to earth will be broken and deflected on contact with those barriers and have a negative effect on him. Whereas, if his aura is pure, bright and powerful, all influences, even evil ones, become beneficial to him.

The third function of the aura is the perception of that which lies concealed in the souls of others and which we experience as impressions of various kinds. Thanks to our aura we may, for instance, feel others either as a chilling draught of cold air that makes us contract, or as a warm, luminous current that causes us to dilate and be glad, and so on.

A strong, healthy aura is the best form of protection we can possibly have. Whatever upheavals the world may go through will leave us unscathed if our aura is pure, luminous and powerful, for it will serve as an insurmountable barrier against every kind of shock, every disturbance of the atmosphere, every manifestation of hatred and every distress. To be surrounded by such an aura, is to be in an impregnable fortress and, when all those around are upset, anxious and demagnetized, he who has such an aura will be full of love and courage, for he will feel that he is inhabited by an inner light. And it is in the power of every one of us to build a strong, effective aura such as this, by means of prayer, meditation and a pure, healthy life and, above all, by the practice of the five virtues that we were talking about a little while ago: kindness, justice, love, wisdom and truth. Each virtue produces its own particular colour and, all together, they give an aura of indescribable richness and splendour.[7]

From the philosophical point of view, the centre signifies the heart, and it is interesting to note that, in certain languages, the words for 'heart', 'lion' and 'love' have the same root. In hebrew the word for heart is *lev* and the word for lion is *lavi;* in Bulgarian and Russian, the word for lion is also *lev,* whereas the word for love is *lubov,* and we find the same root in the English 'love' and the German *Liebe,* which also means love. You know, of course, that the notion of love is always linked to the heart, and Leo (the lion) is the zodiacal sign which is traditionally associated with the heart. The symbol of the circle with the dot in the centre, therefore, stands for the eye, but also for the heart which sends the blood coursing through the body.

If we feel love for somebody, we recognize all kinds of magnificent qualities in him. And if we lose that love, we no longer see all those qualities... even though he may not have changed in any way! It is our heart, therefore, which opens or closes our eyes for us. If we want to know our neighbour, we must love him. Men try to know people and things without loving them, but that is impossible. We can only know others if we warm them with our love so that they open themselves to us. And the same rule applies throughout life. If we don't love nature, she will not allow us to know her. This is the magic secret: to love. Books can give us a great deal of knowledge, but only love allows nature to reveal herself to us. If you want to understand astrology, love the stars, and they will speak to you; if you want to understand precious stones, love them; only your love will enable them to speak to you. Knowledge can never give us the happiness and fulfilment that our hearts and souls are constantly yearning for. Only love can fulfil us and give us happiness. Solomon was versed in every science; the Bible even says that no one could be compared to him in this respect, and yet, in the long run, Solomon declared, *'All is vanity!'* He had hundreds of wives whom he studied assiduously, but he never understood love because love cannot be found in this way.

There are four different ways of looking at love: you can eat it, drink it, breathe it or live it. He who 'eats' love lives on the level of his passions and lowest desires; his heart is never fully satisfied because he is content to remain on the physical level. The attitude of one who 'drinks' love is slightly less crude, but he still restricts himself to the pursuit of pleasure and astral satisfaction. One can also 'breathe' love: certain philosophers, writers and artists breathe love on the mental plane, by their thoughts, but they are few and far between. As for he who lives love, who lives in the subtle, etheric dimension of love, he carries it within him as light in his mind and warmth in his heart, and this light and warmth pour out from him on all around. He who lives in this kind of love is totally fulfilled.

Love is a stream of water flowing from a mountain spring. When Christ said, 'I am the way, the truth, and the life', he was saying: 'I am the fountainhead of truth... I am the river bed in which the water flows... And I am the water itself, the water that is life and love.'[8] The 'way' is the channel down which the waters of life flow and which we can trace back, upstream to the fountainhead of those waters: this channel is wisdom. The fountainhead, therefore, the spring from which the water flows is truth, the channel or path along which it flows is wisdom; and the life, the water which washes over rocks, nourishes plants and quenches the thirst of animals and men, is love. We must love, because, when we love we make it possible for this river, this water of true life, to flow through us and, when this happens it brings many blessings on us.

The mineral kingdom is represented in us by our bones; when we love the stones of the earth it benefits the bone structure of our bodies. When we love plants it benefits our muscular system; by loving animals, we improve our circulatory system; by loving men, we improve the condition of our nervous system, and when we love the angels and the higher beings of the invisible world, we improve the state of our aura, our spiritual organs.

The phenomenon of polarization is present everywhere, throughout the whole of nature. Everything possesses a negative and a positive pole and, in our bodies, our cells are placed according to a harmonious arrangement in which the positive pole of each cell is face to face with the negative pole of its neighbour, and vice versa (Figure 21). When this arrangement is respected we have a sensation of health and physical fitness. If this arrangement is disturbed, however, and the normal pattern of polarization of our cells is no longer respected (Figure 22), we feel ill or uncomfortable. This is how certain feelings such as fear, anger or hatred can suddenly disrupt and disorganize the particles of our body.

Figure 21   Figure 22

The current that flows through our bodies should magnetize the cells in such a way as to polarize them correctly. This explains how magnetism can be used to cure certain illnesses. But if someone who heals through the application of magnetism does not know what he is doing, he can leave his patient feeling more exhausted than ever. One must be full of love in order to heal others; true magnetism is love. Sometimes you will be working away quite quietly when, all of a sudden, for no apparent reason, you begin to feel very tired. This means that a current has touched you and disturbed your magnetism or that, without realizing it, you have had a thought which has cut off the current.

We can magnetize ourselves every day by doing the exercises that I have already demonstrated. Perhaps some of you are a little fearful about this and think, 'That is all very well for Orientals, but not for Westerners.' I can answer your fears by telling you that these methods have been thoroughly tried and tested. Certainly, there are some oriental practices that are dangerous for Westerners, but the exercises I have shown you are very simple and can be assimilated by everyone without danger as easily as bread, water and air! [9]

The passions destroy our inner harmony. I have already talked to you about the diaphragm which constitutes a boundary separating the lungs and heart from the abdomen. But there is another, subtler boundary in man, and that is his solar plexus. We have to see that our solar plexus is fit and able to accomplish this role, otherwise there will be no barrier to prevent harmful elements engendered by our passions from seeping up into our brain. When the solar plexus is strong, it can protect us from all kinds of destructive influences; in doing so it acts in conjunction with the blood which contains elements capable of regenerating the body. We still do not know all the dormant powers of the solar plexus, because our thoughts, feelings and actions continually restrict its action by upsetting the polarization of our cells. In order to have a strong, active solar plexus, therefore, we must be careful not to stir up the lower elements within us; it is they that deprive it of its power to protect us. [10]

Our hearts must be full of love for all human beings, who are our brothers; we should think of them and help them without asking for the least reward. Why? Because we already have our reward; our reward is that tremendous sense of inner fulfilment, the inner warmth and inspiration that floods us when we love. This is, in itself, an immense reward; in fact, life holds none greater. Our thoughts become like a river, a fountain of living water. Human beings are always looking for rewards, but he who truly understands the secret of love no longer looks for any reward; he gives freely because he is perpetually in a state of happiness greater than any that could be imagined. He is immersed in joy; he radiates joy, and this is enough to win him the trust and friendship of countless men and women. What greater reward could there be? Whereas those who launch into interminable discussions and quarrels about the least little thing, cause themselves incalculable damage and loss: they lose their peace and joy; they lose their friends, and they lose their health.

I know that very few will understand me, because, to understand this, one has to be highly evolved and already prepared and capable of doing so. All men are guided by self-interest; no one ever does anything for others unless they expect to get something out of it for themselves as well: they think it would be a waste of time, strength and energy. But the children of God know where truth lies; even at the price of being laughed at and criticized as guileless fools, they would rather live the true life of joy and happiness than have all the wealth in the world, for nothing else can give them that profound inner satisfaction and sense of wonder. And they are not wrong to make this choice, to prefer the love that brings with it the fullness of life; on the contrary: it is the others who are wrong. Believe me, this is true; these things have been verified over and over again by initiates. This is why we, who are the disciples of a great Master, must work with love. We have received freely and we must give freely. Our reward is the joy and happiness we experience at the sight of all those smiling faces and sparkling eyes around us, all those full hearts, all that good will bent on accomplishing splendid actions, all those minds open and ready to study and understand. Tell me: what greater reward could anyone have?

This symbol ⊙, is a daily reminder that we must scale the summits of spiritual mountains. Once we reach the heights, pressure from the outside (our material circumstances) decreases, whereas the thrust of the spirit increases. Spirit and matter, therefore, are both very real, but the fact that matter exists is no reason to let ourselves be crushed by it. The spirit also exists and, if we want it to exist effectively for us, we have to ally ourselves with it. The atmosphere is composed of different layers. The lower layers contain microbes and much dust and decay, but on the higher levels the air becomes purer. Those who have already climbed in high altitudes tell us that, when they find themselves up on the top of a mountain, with peaks all around them, they begin to envisage things differently: their feelings are more disinterested and generous. Some even forget their race and nationality; they feel that they have been lifted above the petty squabbles that divide men. The day will come when we shall rise consciously to higher levels in order to develop qualities of purity, abnegation and greatness of soul.

But you must realize that we too, like the atmosphere, are composed of several different layers and that different kinds of creatures inhabit our different layers. We are under the impression that we are always the same... but that is a delusion! At different moments, great numbers of different beings manifest themselves through us and some of these creatures cannot follow when we rise to higher levels; just as microbes cannot survive if the temperature rises above a certain degree, these creatures cannot breathe above a certain altitude. The higher we go, therefore, the freer we become because, at each step upwards, towards the peaks, many beings of a lower order are obliged to drop off and fall back to their normal level. There is one extraordinarily persistent type of entity, however, which continues to cling to us however high we may go: the entities of pride. All initiates know this: pride is like lichen, it survives on even the highest summits.

We must rise by means of our thoughts. When we pray or meditate we rise, but we can also do so thanks to the efforts we make to improve ourselves. And now (have you noticed?) I am telling you to rise, whereas, only a few moments ago, I was telling you to move towards the centre of the circle. Yes, because, in reality, these two symbols: the centre of the circle and the tip of a cone or mountain, mean exactly the same thing. In nature there is no such thing as up or down, left or right. These terms simply express the rapidity or the sluggishness and the greater or lesser amplitude of our vibrations. Height and centredness correspond to rapid vibrations; lowness and outwardness correspond to slow vibrations. Thoughts, feelings and acts can also be seen on the scale of vibrations: the passions of avarice, jealousy, anger, fear and envy correspond to slow, weak vibrations. You will say that fear is not slow, it is very rapid. Yes, outwardly it is rapid, but inwardly it paralyses thought and makes one incapable of action. It frequently happens that, when a house is on fire, for instance, instead of escaping, people rush into the flames! Yes, because fear makes them lose their heads. Harmonious thoughts and feelings, on the contrary, are conducive to easy, rapid and effective action.

The Master Peter Deunov wrote a book about colour. In it, he explained that it is the angels that rule colour and that everything that takes place in nature takes place with the help of the colours that are at work in plants, animals and men. I have read a great many things in this book; among others, the Master says that when we pronounce certain verses of the Bible out loud, they produce certain colours around us and that we can use these colours to heal someone who is ill, by reading them aloud to them. Turkish hakims also heal the sick by reading verses of the Koran to them.

The Master used to say, 'You want to wrest the secrets of nature from her, but nature is alive; she knows you and she knows how often you have been ungrateful, so she hides from you. Nature amuses ordinary men, she teaches disciples, but she unveils her secrets only to sages. Everything in nature possesses form, content and meaning. The form is for ordinary human beings; the content is for disciples, and the deep meaning is for masters.' Everyone thinks they can delve into the great mysteries of nature, but that is not so easy. Special preparation is needed before being capable of understanding them, and this preparation is only achieved by the practice of the five virtues we spoke about earlier. Kindness sets us in motion and, as we progress along the way of initiation, enables us to observe and experience all the beautiful things that God has created. Justice enables us to act and create works of beauty with our hands. Love inspires the words that restore life; it enables us to taste and enjoy all that is most appetizing in nature and, in this way, to feel continually nourished and refreshed by living waters. Wisdom opens our spiritual ears; one day, thanks to wisdom, we shall hear the music of the spheres and understand the divine Word. Truth sets us on the right path and enables us to get our bearings and find what we are looking for, to contemplate the beauty of nature and the countenance of Ain Soph, the ancient of ancients, the mystery of mysteries of which the Cabbalah speaks.

It is amazing to see how most human beings think that they will be allowed to penetrate the mysteries of the highest Initiations without putting anything into practice, while they continue to indulge all their weaknesses and refuse to make the slightest sacrifice or effort to gain the mastery of themselves. This is why the secrets of nature are hidden from them and sealed with seven seals. Remember what the Master said: 'Nature amuses ordinary men, she teaches disciples, but she unveils her secrets only to sages.'

I had also intended to explain some points of phrenology today, but there is very little time left for that. However, I want you to look at this sketch of a head (Figure 23):

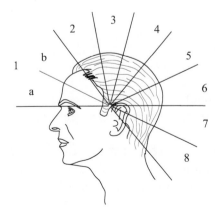

Figure 23

The first division is sub-divided into two parts: the first (a), corresponds to the love of concrete, tangible things, to science; the upper part of the forehead (b) corresponds to the love of abstract things, to philosophy. The second division corresponds to love of others, to benevolence, altruism and humanitarian tendencies. The third division corresponds to love of God, devotion and a spirit of veneration for higher beings. The fourth division indicates someone who has a strong, obstinate attachment to his personal convictions and opinions. If this region of the skull is overdeveloped in relation to the other regions, it indicates someone who would let himself be burned alive rather than renounce his convictions. The fifth division corresponds to love of self, to self-esteem. The sixth division corresponds to love of house and country; the seventh, to love of children and family, and the eighth corresponds to the instincts.

We are told that Paradise was a garden full of trees and animals of every sort and kind. In this garden, Eve was the first botanist of the human race because she took care of the plants and flowers, whereas Adam was the first zoologist; it was he who named the animals.

From the esoteric point of view, the sun represents the first man: Adam. The Bible tells us that Eve was formed from one of Adam's ribs.[11] This is true, because a sliver of the sun's disc gives us the moon (Figure 24). The sun is the masculine principle and the moon the feminine principle. The union of these two principles produces Mercury (Figure 25), child of sun and moon. But Mercury is not Adam and Eve's first-born: before Mercury, came Cain (Mars) and Abel (Venus). The sun and moon are the two principles, masculine and feminine, which unite to give birth to the four elements. For alchemists, the union of the sun and moon is symbolized by the sign of Mercury ☿ which contains and represents the four elements, two of which are masculine and two feminine. The crescent of the moon ☽ represents water; the sun ☉ represents fire; + is the sign of their union, the earth; and Mercury itself ☿ represents air.

Figure 24   Figure 25

And there is yet another way to interpret the symbol of the sun. Imagine an orange: the skin of the orange is wisdom; the part that we eat is love, and the seeds that we plant are truth.[12]

We must live in love, for love is the only thing that enables us to rise to a higher level. The nature of your love is a sure indication of the destiny that awaits you for, sooner or later, you will be given whatever you love. You may say that you have already loved a great many things and that you have never received any of them! Don't worry; they will come! What we have today is what we once loved, in former incarnations. If our love is turned towards the spiritual world, so much the better, for we shall attract it to us. Wherever our love is today, there shall we be tomorrow. If our love is inferior, it will drag us down to hell; our destiny depends on our love.

And now, in concluding this informal conversation that we have been having together, let me say that I hope with all my heart that you will think deeply about the truths that I have put to you in the simplest possible terms. I have chosen to use this form because I trust that you will not be misled by appearances and that, instead of dispersing your energies in a host of unimportant details, you will discover, hidden behind these simple words, solutions to the essential problems of your lives. My hope is that, very often, as often as possible, you will scale this sacred mountain, this solar mountain, and that, from its summit your gaze may embrace a vast horizon. United by bonds of spiritual love, we shall continue these experiences together and you will see that your lives will change from day to day.

May the river of living water bring life to the trees and flowers of your inner gardens!

Paris, 12 February 1938

Notes

1. See *The Symbolic Language of Geometrical Figures,* Izvor Coll. n° 218, chap. 4: 'The Pentagram'.
2. Op. cit., chap. 2: 'The Circle'.
3. See *The Philosopher's Stone – in the Gospels and in Alchemy,* Izvor Coll. n° 241, chap. 10: 'The philosopher's stone, fruit of a mystic union', and chap. 14: 'The gold of true knowledge: the alchemist and the gold prospector'.
4. See *The Mysteries of Yesod – Foundations of the Spiritual Life,* Complete Works, vol. 7, Part II, chap. 10: 'Blessed are the Pure in Heart' and *Looking into the Invisible – Intuition, Clairvoyance, Dreams,* Izvor Coll. n° 228, chap. 10: 'The Spiritual Eye'.
5. See *Man's Psychic Life: Elements and Structures,* Izvor Coll. n° 222, chap. 13: 'The Higher Self'.
6. See *Cosmic Moral Law,* Complete Works, vol. 12, chap. 5: 'The Law of Affinity: Peace'.
7. See *Notre peau spirituelle, l'aura,* Brochure n° 309.
8. See *Truth: Fruit of Wisdom and Love,* Izvor Coll. n° 234, chap. 6: 'I am the Way, the Truth and the Life'.
9. See *A New Earth – Methods, exercises, formulas, prayers,* Complete Works, vol. 13, Appendix: 'The physical exercises'.
10. See *Man's Subtle Bodies and Centres – the Aura, the Solar Plexus, the Chakras...,* Izvor Coll. n° 219, chap. 3: 'The Solar Plexus'.
11. See *Cosmic Balance – The Secret of Polarity,* Izvor Coll. n° 237, chap. 4: 'The Role of The Masculine and The Feminine: Adam and Eve: Spirit and Matter'.
12. See *Truth: Fruit of Wisdom and Love,* Izvor Coll. n° 234, chap. 5: 'Truth, the Kernel of Life'.

Chapter Four

WISDOM IS HIDDEN IN THE EARS

'Very truly, I tell you, anyone who hears my word and believes him who sent me has eternal life, and does not come under judgement, but has passed from death to life. Very truly, I tell you, the hour is coming, and is now here, when the dead will hear the voice of the Son of God, and those who hear will live.

John 5, 24-25

As I have already told you, man and the whole of nature is a living Gospel. What profound science is hidden in our physical body with all its organs! What a wealth of things we would find in it if only we understood it!

In my last lecture, I talked to you about the eyes and this geometrical figure ☉, which symbolizes the eye. This evening I want to talk to you about the ears.

Christ said, *'Very truly, I tell you, the hour is coming, and is now here, when the dead will hear the voice of the Son of God, and those who hear will live.'* We all have ears but we very rarely think about what they represent. Anatomists know all about the structure of the ear, how it functions and how it enables us to hear sounds, but their knowledge goes no further. But if we studied the hidden laws that govern the way the ears function, we would have a better perception of the profound wisdom with which the Creator has built our organ of hearing.

We possess five sense organs, each of which perceives a particular aspect of matter. The sense of touch perceives solid matter and the sense of taste, liquid matter. You will object that we can taste sugar and yet it is solid. Yes, it starts by being solid, but wc can only taste it when our saliva begins to melt it. We cannot taste anything unless it is liquid. The sense of smell perceives gaseous emanations, which are also a state of matter. With the sense of hearing we leave the world of dense matter and enter that of waves and vibrations, and, finally, with the sense of sight, we reach an even subtler world, almost the etheric world. From taste to sight, therefore, we see that there is a difference of hierarchy between the different senses which are designed for progressively subtler perceptions.

The five senses are the children of the skin.[1] Primitive forms of animal life which had neither ears nor eyes, perceived the outside world and orientated themselves by means of their skin. Later, the functions of the skin became differentiated and organs of hearing, smell and sight appeared. The skin still possesses hidden possibilities which will manifest themselves in the future.

The five senses, therefore, are designed to put us in touch with solid, liquid, gaseous, aerial and etheric elements. This means that touch is related to the physical body, taste to the astral body and the nose to the lower mental body, the intellect. A student of physiognomy can tell a person's intellectual tendencies from the shape of his nose, and his emotional tendencies from the shape of his mouth. As for the ears, they represent the higher mental body, the Causal body, whereas the eyes represent the divine body.

The Bible often mentions man's ears. For example, *'They have ears but do not hear'*, or *'Those who have ears to hear, let them hear.'*

As you know, the ear is divided into three parts: the outer ear or pinna, the middle ear and the inner ear. This division corresponds to the three worlds: physical, astral (which makes transmission possible) and mental or spiritual. Of the outer ear, I shall say only that it reveals a person's character. It, too, is divided into three distinct parts (Figure 26): the helix which represents the mind; the antihelix, which represents the heart, and the lobe which represents the instincts, material tastes and physical appetites (greed and sensuality).

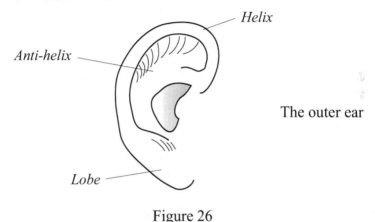

Figure 26

Every detail of a person's strengths and weaknesses are written in the outer ear: each line or fold is extraordinarily significant. In fact, one can even tell how long a person will live, from his ears. Perhaps, if the great criminologist, Cesare Lombroso, were here, he would find that we all showed criminal tendencies! As a matter of fact, some very highly advanced people sometimes have ears that denote degeneracy. This is because the ears, like the eyes, the forehead, the nose, mouth and chin, represent a bank:[2] a person can have a great deal of money in one bank and little or none in another. If someone's ears are not well made, therefore, we must not necessarily conclude that he is vicious or stupid; it may be that, in the past, he neglected to develop certain qualities and virtues. We must be very prudent in drawing conclusions.

And now, let us see how the ear is constructed:

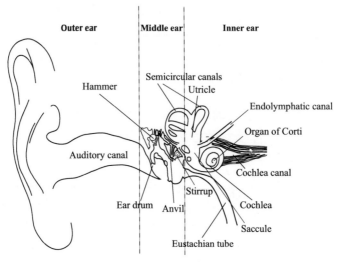

Figure 27

The outer ear or pinna, is connected to the ear drum or tympanum by the auditory canal (twenty-four millimetres in length). Within the tympanum is the chain of three small bones (hammer, anvil and stirrup) which transmit sound to the inner ear. But what we are particularly interested in today is the inner ear, consisting of:

1 – the bony labyrinth containing the semicircular canals, aligned at right angles to each other on the three planes of space, and whose role is to ensure bodily equilibrium, and the cochlea with its three spiral coils.

2 – the membranous labyrinth which, with the utricle and the saccule, contains the watery fluid known as endolymph (this fluid is also present in the semicircular canals, the endolymphatic canal and the cochlea) in which float minute grains of calcareous matter which also contribute to maintaining bodily equilibrium.

The membranous labyrinth terminates in the organ of Corti, and it is this that is, properly speaking, the auditory organ. The organ of Corti can be compared to a harp; it is composed of thousands (24,000) of flexible fibres like the vibrant strings of a musical instrument.

Astrology tells us that the ears are governed by Saturn and, hearing the name of Saturn, some of you may feel a little uneasy, because astrologers also tell us, when any great upheaval occurs on earth – epidemics, floods or earthquakes, for instance – that it was caused by Saturn. That is true. And yet, Saturn is a magnificent planet and if it influences us negatively, it is because its currents encounter certain elements in our aura which distort and deform them and render them harmful. The truth is that Saturn can give us magnificent qualities: sages, initiates, ascetics, hermits and philosophers possess all the good qualities of Saturn. Without Saturn one can have neither power nor tenacity, neither patience, endurance nor stability.

All the glyphs used in astrology are composed – with occasional slight modifications in shape – from those of the Sun ☉, the Moon ☽ and the Earth ♁ . The glyphs of all the planets: Mercury, Mars, Venus, Jupiter, Saturn, Uranus and Neptune are simply combinations of these three principles: Sun, Moon and Earth. The Sun represents the divine world, the Moon the astral, psychic world and the Earth the physical, material world. Mercury ☿, as you see, has the Sun in the centre, the Moon above and the Earth below. Venus ♀ has the Sun above and the Earth below. Mars ♂ has the same elements as Venus but in reverse. The glyph for Jupiter ♃ consists of the Moon above and the Earth below. The glyph for Saturn ♄ is the reverse of Jupiter. The glyph for Uranus ♅ is composed of the glyphs of the Sun, the Earth and two glyphs of the Moon, and that of Neptune ♆ is the same, except for a slight modification of the Moon and the Earth. I shall not expand on the esoteric meaning of these glyphs today, but I want to say just a few words about Saturn.

Greek mythology tells us that Saturn was the son of Uranus (Ouranos in Greek), heaven, and of Gaea, the Earth. But astrology tells us that Saturn rules the two signs of Capricorn and Aquarius. Capricorn is an earth sign and Aquarius an air sign. In Cancer and Leo, the opposite signs to Capricorn and Aquarius, Saturn is in fall. But Cancer is the house of the Moon and Leo is the house of the Sun, and this is why the qualities of Saturn are the reverse of those of Sun and Moon.

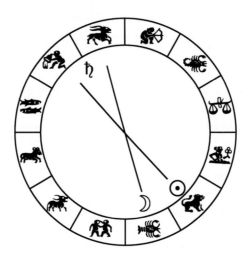

Figure 28

As we have seen, the glyph for Saturn ♄ is the reverse of that of Jupiter ♃. In the beginning, according to legend, Saturn was master of the universe, but he became so proud, unjust and cruel that he devoured even his own children. Saturn's spouse, Rhea, saved Jupiter from his father's clutches by a trick and, when Jupiter grew up, he dethroned his father and took his place.

The influence of Saturn can be seen in different areas of nature, but we must first look at how it manifests itself in man. From the point of view of phrenology, Saturn is associated with the centres on the forehead which correspond to love of knowledge, reasoning and reflection, but also with the centre at the back of the skull which corresponds to stability and perseverance and even to obstinacy. Wisdom is Saturn's most excellent quality, for he is the oldest of the planets and has the advantage of experience. Saturn is also associated with the liver. Astrologers say that the liver is ruled by Jupiter and the lungs by Saturn. This was true in the beginning: Jupiter was in the liver and Saturn in the lungs, but when Jupiter rebelled against his father, he took over the government of the lungs and relegated Saturn to the liver. The Bulgarian name for the liver is ceren drob, which means 'black lung' and the lungs themselves are called bel drob, 'white lung'. And this is what we see depicted in the glyphs of these two planets: one is the right way round ♃ and the other is reversed ♄ .

Tradition portrays Saturn digging and working in mines and underground places; he is often shown as a bearded old man, wielding a pickaxe. This is an image of the work he does in the liver. Saturn also rules the teeth and the skeleton. Certain animals come under the influence of Saturn; some of them, such as moles and rats, live underground or in holes, whereas others, such as bats and owls, prefer to come out at night. The ass is also ruled by Saturn and is a very important symbol. But I must not take the time, now, to look at Saturn's influence in plants and stones; we have more important things to study.

Saturn represents the old Adam; the Sun represents the new Adam, the Christ. The old Adam disobeyed God's orders in the garden of Eden. God had said, *'You may freely eat of every tree of the garden; but of the tree of the knowledge of good and evil you shall not eat'*. But Saturn (Adam), wanting to become as powerful as God himself, disobeyed God's command, and it was this act of disobedience that overthrew him and sent him hurtling to earth, where he was condemned to toil and earn his bread in the sweat of his brow. In other words, Saturn fell headlong into the liver which, in this context, signifies purgatory or hell. The liver is the physical body's most important factory; it is here that all the toxins of the body are transformed and bile is manufactured.

Now, look at these two sketches (Figure 29):

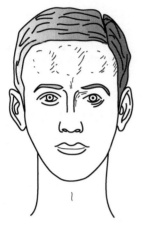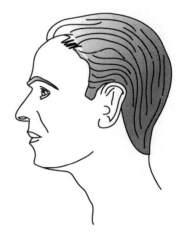

Figure 29

The good qualities of Saturn are situated in the middle of the forehead; these are an aptitude for philosophy, the ability to grasp the contents of ideas and to make comparisons and, on the top of the head and slightly to the rear of the forehead, are the centres of perseverance, stability and endurance. I have mentioned the ability to make comparisons, and I would like to say a few words about this: the ability to make comparisons is one of the most important faculties we possess, because it enables us to understand the analogies that exist between the different levels of nature.[3] You are all familiar with the Emerald Tablet which says, 'That which is below is like to that which is above'. This is a comparison. And when Jesus said, *'Your will be done, on earth as it is in heaven'*, this, too, was a comparison: the idea that the earth should be like heaven. Of course, there is a great deal to be said about comparisons, but I shall limit myself to only a few remarks.

Saturnians, or rather, those of them who are not very highly evolved, keep their eyes fixed on the ground. This is not a good habit for, when man looks at what is below him and compares himself to what he sees (when he compares himself, for instance, to those who are ignorant and foolish), he is bound to think, 'I am more intelligent, wiser and more learned than them', and he is led to despise them. If we compare ourselves to something too small, to microbes or ants, of course, we shall see ourselves as giants, and from there it is only a step to being devoured by pride, and pride is a tremendous handicap on the path of evolution. But if we compare ourselves to initiates or other beings of a very high calibre, far more highly evolved than ourselves, then we shall immediately see that we are neither very kind nor intelligent nor worthy of respect. When someone recognizes how small he really is, it makes for humility, and he becomes gentler and more indulgent and his desire to grow and advance to greater heights begins to develop. Saturnians who are not aware of this danger can misuse their capacity for comparison and fall into the trap of pride: this is why they are so often embroiled in intrigue, suspicion and revenge. If we want to become luminous and kind, we must compare ourselves to the sons of light.

Perseverance, stability and great powers of endurance are some of Saturn's most excellent qualities. Jesus rode into Jerusalem on the back of a she-ass, and this is a symbol. Many people have a very poor opinion of asses, in spite of their very fine qualities: they are very sober, even ascetical, and can survive on very little. In fact, they even eat thorns! The patience of a donkey is inexhaustible... and its obstinacy also! You laugh at that, but, I assure you, donkeys merit your respect! It is very insulting to the animal to say, as is the custom in Bulgaria, that a drunkard drinks like an ass. An ass drinks only water; in fact it will drink only pure water, and it is perfectly capable of knowing whether it is pure or not. This is truly a very remarkable quality. If you need pure water, let your donkey lead you to its own supply and you may be sure that it will be pure.

The liver is a very important gland whose health is largely dependent on what we eat, but also on our thoughts and feelings.[4]

When we eat too much or not enough, or if we eat impure food, the liver feels the ill effects and is unable to fulfil its function properly and, when this happens, it can no longer defend our organism against invasion by poisons. The liver is very sensitive to what we eat, and it does not like meat. You think that it is just the contrary, but you are wrong. When animals sense that they are being led to the slaughter, you cannot imagine what hatred they feel for men and the terror and anguish they experience! They have no way of expressing these feelings, but that does not prevent them from experiencing them, and their secretions become virulent poisons which impregnate every cell of their bodies. This means that, when we eat meat, however well all this is disguised by delicious seasoning, that is what we are eating: poison. And it is a poison that is more psychic than physical, for it was caused by the animal's suffering and transmitted through its vibrations to its physical glands. When we eat meat, the fluids it contains are also taken into our bodies and absorbed by the liver. If a person's liver is not in good condition, he will have a tendency to be worried and anxious. Discontent, pessimism and anxiety are all related to disorders of the liver. There have been many philosophers who suffered from disorders of the liver.

From the astrological point of view, my country, Bulgaria, represents the liver of Europe, whereas France represents its heart. The liver and the heart are both vital organs and, if we are to believe what astrology tells us, this means that the destiny of Europe will depend to a great extent on that of its heart and liver: France and Bulgaria. The question that interests us here is the spiritual dimension of these two countries; they will both have an immense role to play in this respect in the future.

If we want to improve the health of our whole organism, we should take care of our liver by eating pure food and living a pure life. You will probably laugh if I tell you, for example, that if you drink a cup of well boiled hot water every morning on an empty stomach, it will purify your organism. Hot water is the most natural and harmless and, at the same time, the most potent remedy there is. We continually accumulate wastes in the body, and these wastes can only be eliminated by fasting and drinking hot water. Some people, when they sweat, like to cool themselves down with a glass of cold, or even iced, water. But, apart from the fact that this is a dangerous habit, cold water makes the blood vessels contract and slows the circulation. Hot water, on the contrary, causes the tissues to expand, thereby improving the circulation. Try it and you will see how many ills, including migraine, loss of appetite and insomnia, can be avoided or cured thanks to the regular use of hot water. It possesses all the properties needed to purify the body. The minerals that are always present to a greater or lesser degree in cold water leave deposits on the walls of the arteries, thus causing arteriosclerosis and the hardening of the arteries. When you drink hot water it dissolves these calcareous deposits and the tissues regain their elasticity.

Only those who understand things from the spiritual point of view will accept what I am going to say: the others will be unable to do so. Hot water can be looked on as a teacher. It says to our cells, 'You must be gentle, friendly and obedient and full of warmth and kindness...' And the love in our cells increases; the heat causes them to expand and they begin to accept the teaching of love which is inseparable from warmth. Cold says just the opposite: 'Contract, be selfish and disobedient...' Cold believes in self-centredness and a harsh, chilly attitude; this is what it teaches our cells. Some of you may say, 'For heaven's sake... What a ridiculous way to look at things!' And yet, this is what the actual experiences of life teach.

This does not mean that we must never drink cold or iced drinks, particularly in hot countries. But, even there, if you drink something hot when the weather is very hot, you will feel extraordinarily refreshed. To be sure, in the summer, a cold drink is pleasanter and, for a short time, at least, it is refreshing, but it will not prevent you from suffering from the heat; in fact, it will leave you even more enervated by it. Another thing I want to tell you, is that if you have a temperature, you can bring it down by drinking three or four cups of boiling water. When you catch a cold or a chill, before taking any medication, try drinking several cups of very hot, well boiled water.

Men possess two kinds of knowledge: that which, as it were, belongs to them and that which is foreign to them. Even the greatest philosopher on earth, if his knowledge is purely theoretical – in other words, if he has never put it into practice or verified it in his own life – will be an ignoramus in his next incarnation; he will be deprived of all his former knowledge. Whereas the most insignificant little man who tries to put into practice what he knows in the domain of the virtues, will come back endowed with true intelligence and wisdom and a rich store of innate possibilities. I see a great many people in this world who were renowned as great scholars in the past but who, today, have forgotten all they ever knew. But the knowledge of what you actually experience in life will remain yours, and, whatever planet you go to in the future, you will take it with you. All the other kinds of knowledge, all the theories and book-learning that you have borrowed from others, will be obliterated and lost to you. How many people realize the truth of all this?

Let me say a little more about this question of the experiences we need to have in life. Some people have no hesitation in throwing themselves into all kinds of dangerous adventures or impure or perverse pleasures, on the pretext that it would be a lack of broad-mindedness and intellectual curiosity not to experience them for themselves. But when it comes to experiences of a higher order, they are content to quote others: 'Buddha, Moses, Plato or Jesus said thus and so'! In this area, they do nothing to put their declarations to the test and experience them for themselves, as they do for things which are liable to defile and corrupt them. They experiment with every form of error or passion, every form of pleasure whether licit or illicit, every conceivable form of vice or crime, on the pretext that they want to know all there is to know and taste life to the full. But how much longer will they go on invoking the same excuse and experiencing all that they they have already experienced so many times in past incarnations? If they continue to seek experience on this level, they will also continue to be incapable of understanding experiences of a higher order in the domain of love, wisdom and truth.

You must understand that it is not enough to go on and on for ever, repeating the experience of the lower worlds; that there is another, higher realm to be explored and enjoyed: the magnificent, luminous realm of a higher order of experience capable of freeing man from the grip of error, darkness and suffering. The initiates refuse to go on repeating these age-old errors. In these matters, they quote from the experience of others. It is enough for them if others are drunkards, perverts or criminals; they don't need to imitate them and experience these things for themselves in order to understand them. But when it comes to the experience of the divine, they are not content to know that Jesus, St Paul or St John had such experiences: they want to experience them for themselves.

There are two kinds of Saturnians, therefore: those who seek the magnificent experiences of a higher order, and those who live in the domain of the liver and who experiment with poisons. It is obviously preferable to experiment with the higher realms and to be content to quote the experiences of others for what concerns the lower worlds.

And now, let's get back to the subject of the ears. We have already seen that the organ of equilibrium is in the inner ear. But what is equilibrium? There are three kinds of equilibrium: stable, unstable and indeterminate. Suppose that we hang an oblong object from one end: the point at which it is attached being higher than its centre of gravity, the object will be in a state of stable equilibrium; if it is knocked off balance it will automatically regain its equilibrium of its own accord. However, if we suspend a similar object from a point below its centre of gravity, it will be in a state of unstable equilibrium; if it is knocked off balance it cannot regain it of its own accord. And, finally, if we attach something at its centre of gravity (the point of suspension and the centre of gravity being one and the same) it will always be in a state of equilibrium whatever its position. This is what we call indeterminate equilibrium.

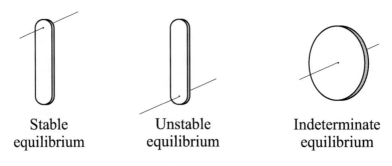

Stable	Unstable	Indeterminate
equilibrium	equilibrium	equilibrium

Figure 30

These three forms of equilibrium can be found within ourselves. In the first case – that of stable equilibrium – the pivot or point of attachment is the head, and the centre of gravity is the stomach. Only he who believes that reason and wisdom take priority over material possessions can maintain a state of stable equilibrium because he is firmly attached to a philosophy. He is content to put his food into his centre of gravity. Beings such as this, of course, are not immune from suffering and difficulty in their lives, but they are always capable of getting back onto an even keel.

The pivotal point of one who gives priority to pleasure, food and the passions, on the other hand, is on the level of his stomach, whereas his centre of gravity is in his head. He is in a perpetually unstable position, always liable to lose his balance at the first sign of difficulty, and unable to recover it. The drunkard whose head is his centre of gravity and whose stomach is his point of attachment is a living example of this as he staggers home, reeling from side to side!

As for those whose lives are guided by intuition and the inner voice, they are in a state of equilibrium comparable to the equilibrium of the earth as it rotates round the sun: their point of attachment and their centre of gravity coincide in the solar plexus, the ultimate centre of both intuition and equilibrium.

True equilibrium cannot be found in fragile, changeable reality symbolized by earth or water. Picture a man and woman, each in their own little boat, out at sea: they sail along side by side and exchange promises of eternal love and fidelity. 'I love you and I'll love you for ever!' says one, and the other replies, 'I love you. I swear to be true and never forsake you.' But the wind gets up and separates those two little boats. As he is being carried away by the waves, the man shouts, 'You are unfaithful!' and the woman replies, 'No, it's you who has failed me.' Neither of them is guilty, but their promises were based on water.

The membranous labyrinth of the ear is composed of rows of minute fibres or cilia which can be compared to the strings of a musical instrument. Pick up a violin and make one of its strings vibrate by plucking it from where it rests on the bridge and then letting it snap back. The sound will be all the louder if you pull the string a long way from its original position. The intensity of the sound changes according to the distance; the note itself is still the same, however. But if you shorten the string and again make it vibrate, you will find that the pitch is no longer the same; you get a higher note. Now take another instrument, a guitar, for instance: if you pluck a string on the guitar and on the violin alternately, you will notice a difference in the timbre or quality of tone. We see, therefore, that sound possesses three essential characteristics: loudness or intensity, pitch and timbre or quality, all of which can be distinguished by the organ of Corti. Loudness, or intensity, depends on the amplitude of vibrations; pitch depends on the frequency, that is to say, the number of vibrations in any fixed length of time (the higher the frequency, the higher the pitch), and timbre depends on the nature of the instrument.

The ability to distinguish sounds is Saturn's finest quality. Initiates tell us that the universe is one vast symphony that defies description, and the student of astrology can understand this symphony if he knows the intensity, the pitch and the timbre, because the intensity indicates the strength of the physical elements, the pitch indicates the moral qualities and the timbre reveals the nature of the elements present. With the assistance of these data, we can now see what a horoscope is. In a birth chart we have planets, signs and houses.

1. The timbre is the planet. Each planet, Jupiter, Saturn, Venus, etc. possesses its own characteristics, its own particular nature.

2. The pitch is the zodiacal sign in which a planet is situated and which enables it to manifest its best or its worst qualities as the case may be.

3. The house in which the planet is found determines the strength or intensity with which it manifests itself.

The position of the planets in the signs indicates a person's psychic qualities. Their position in the houses indicates how he will manifest these qualities on the physical plane. If the planet is in a good sign and a bad house, it cannot manifest itself on the physical level in its own particular domain, in spite of all its good qualities. On the other hand, a planet may be in fall or in detriment in a sign, but if it is in a good house, even if it does not possess very good qualities, it can manifest itself on the physical plane, in its own domain. This often happens, and it leads people to think that someone is very gifted when, in fact, he is not. Take the example of someone who has Jupiter in Sagittarius or Pisces in the twelfth house: even if he possesses very outstanding qualities, they will remain hidden; whereas if someone has Jupiter in Gemini or Virgo in the tenth house, his qualities will always be recognized and shown off to advantage.

When I speak of good or bad houses, I am not saying that the houses are, in themselves, either good or bad. But, depending on which planets are concerned, they can be more or less favourable.

If you have Jupiter in the second house, for instance (the house of possessions and money), he will have a favourable influence on your financial situation, whereas Saturn in the second house will have a distinctly unfavourable influence or, at any rate, any good effects will be delayed. The possible combinations of the ten planets that have been discovered so far (and others will be discovered in the years to come) with the twelve constellations and twelve houses, are incalculable. In addition, there are important geometrical relationships between planets. These are what astrologers call 'aspects', and they, too, have to be taken into consideration. The aspects represent the angle between two planets measured in degrees on the ecliptic.

The essential aspects are as follows:

Trine △, sextile ✶, semi-sextile ⊻, conjunction ☌, opposition ☍, square ☐ and semi-square L.

Trines (120°), sextiles (60°) and semi-sextiles (30°) are traditionally said to be harmonious and favourable.

Oppositions (180°), squares (90°) and semi-squares (45°) are said to be inharmonious and unfavourable.

An angle of conjunction of less than 10° is also said to be extremely strong and significant; whether it is favourable or unfavourable depends on the planets involved.

Intensity, pitch and timbre can also be seen in the aspects. Take any aspect: its timbre depends on the two planets involved; its pitch depends on the two zodiacal signs in which they are placed, and its intensity depends on the houses in which the aspect is situated. My task, this evening, is not to explain astrology to you, but to give you some keys to it. We talk about heavenly harmony, but without knowing that the fundamental laws of this harmony are hidden in our ears, in the organ of Corti.

As I have already said, the essential quality of Saturn is his power of discernment. The sage is capable of discerning intensity from pitch and timbre, wolves from sheep, bees from wasps, springs from swamps, the spiritual from the material. This is wisdom: the ability to discern each thing at every moment.

Yes, just as there is a third eye, which we have already talked about, there is a third ear, which is developed by initiates and clairaudients. This third ear is in the throat, on the level of the thyroid gland. In order to develop it, one has to be capable of living in silence. In the past, initiates, ascetics and hermits retired to live in solitude in order to listen to that inner voice. Like Saturn, they remained alone the better to hear... If you want to hear that inner voice, enter into yourself and listen to it.

You can tell the difference between someone who is wise and someone who is not, simply by observing how they listen. To listen is a science in itself. We all think that we are capable of listening, but that is not so; very few people know how to listen and those who do are true Saturnians. They say very little but they listen.

I have said that we should be capable of distinguishing wolves from sheep and wasps from bees... but we sometimes prefer intensity to pitch and say, admiringly: 'Yes, he's a wolf, to be sure, but he is so strong!' And we surrender to the wolf. Sheep are weak, that is true, but they are more highly evolved than wolves. The future does not hold great promise for wolves; nobody is prepared to feed them or give them a home, on the contrary; everybody is ready to pursue and kill them. Whereas sheep have a bright future ahead of them because they are capable of giving; bees, too. Misers will receive nothing.

There was once an old miser who died and found himself in hell. Some angels who saw him there, were sorry for him and went to talk to St Peter to see if there was not something they could do to help him. St Peter agreed to search in his ledger to see if the miser had done at least one good deed in his life and, sure enough, he found that, a long time ago, he had given a black radish to a beggar. This was enough for the angels, who went and got the radish and let it down into hell on the end of a string. When he saw the radish hanging in front of him, the miser clutched at it and, immediately, St Peter and the angels began to pull it up again, with the miser hanging on for dear life. But there were other souls in hell who saw this and thought that they could escape, too, if they clung to his legs. But the miser could not bear to let anyone else take advantage of his unexpected rescue; kicking out in a fury, he shouted: 'Let go of my legs; it's my radish!' Immediately, the string broke and they all tumbled back into hell. And the moral of this little story is that we should not be like that miser and refuse to share our good fortune, otherwise we shall certainly fall down into hell.

True Saturnians are those who know how to listen to the voice of God. You will ask, 'How does the voice of God make itself heard? How can I listen to it?'[5] When the Prophet Elijah fled from Jezebel, he hid for a long time in the desert and the voice of the Lord came to him there. *'And behold the Lord passed by, and a great and strong wind tore into the mountains and broke the rocks in pieces before the Lord, but the Lord was not in the wind; and after the wind an earthquake, but the Lord was not in the earthquake; and after the earthquake a fire, but the Lord was not in the fire; and after the fire a still small voice.'* The voice of the Lord was not in the storm, nor in the earthquake, nor in the fire; it was in the murmur of *'a still small voice'*. Yes, the voice of God is barely audible; that is why you have to be very attentive if you want to hear it.

The Prophet Jonah also heard the voice of God; it said to him: *'Go at once to Nineveh, that great city, and cry out against it; for their wickedness has come up before me.'* But Jonah was frightened and did not want to go to Nineveh, so he embarked on a ship bound for Tarshish. When they were out at sea, the ship was caught in a great storm and the terrified sailors cast lots to find out who was responsible for the storm. The lot fell on Jonah and he was thrown overboard and swallowed by a whale. Jonah spent three days in the belly of the whale and, during those three days, he thought over what had happened to him and finally called on the Lord to forgive him and promised to do what he had commanded. Then the whale vomited Jonah onto dry land

and he was saved. Like Jonah, when we don't want to do what the voice of God asks of us, we meet a whale, and then we have to stay in its belly for several days. How many whales do we meet in our lifetime? Many, of all different sizes and shapes and colours. If we were more attentive, we should hear that still, small voice that always speaks to us before we commit ourselves to something important, whether it be a journey, a new job or any other important decision; but we don't listen. We are too fond of noise and violent winds, and this means that any being who wants to make himself heard has to make a lot of noise; if he speaks softly we don't listen.

And yet, it is important for you to know that when entities of a higher order speak to us, they say no more than a few words and their voice is almost inaudible. Sometimes, when we have had an accident, we think back and realize that it was our own fault. We say to ourselves, 'Yes; I should have known. Something warned me, but it spoke so softly, so softly...' We didn't listen; we preferred to listen to the loud, insistent voices that led us into error. God speaks softly, without insisting: He says something once, twice, perhaps three times, but no more. And the same is true of intuition, so if we don't listen very attentively, if we fail to hear that small voice because of our fondness for noise, violence and great storms, we shall constantly be led astray.[6] The voice of heaven is extremely soft, tender, melodious and brief. He who desires our good, who has been sent to us by God, manifests himself in three ways: by the light which he causes to dawn within us, by a feeling of warmth, a sense of expansion and love in our hearts and by a sensation of liberty and the decision to act with nobility and disinterestedness.

You may be sure that he who seeks to enlighten your mind, warm your heart and free your will, whether he be rich or poor, learned or ignorant, is a messenger from God. But keep well away from anyone who creates confusion within you, who limits you, causes your heart to contract and robs you of the will to accomplish something intelligent and beautiful. Avoid anyone who has this effect on you; don't trust him, even if he is the most learned, renowned and illustrious of men, for he can only spell disaster for you; he will bring every possible misfortune on you.

Saturn has no love for the proud, the unjust and the dishonest; he has no use for those who let wealth, fame or pleasure turn their heads. He turns everything upside down and destroys everything; he serves as a kind of customs officer in nature, at the frontier of the septenary. To the traveller who approaches his customs house at the border, Saturn asks, 'What have you come here for? There is too much pride in you; your wealth overburdens you; I cannot let you cross the border.' No one who is not pure is allowed to cross the border. Saturn is the guardian of the threshold and it is he, also, who is keeper of the archives. Yes, the archives of the world and of the history of mankind are in the custody of Saturn; he is nature's greatest archivist. It is he who is the keeper of all knowledge, who knows everything and records it all in the causal world. But we shall only be allowed to read the archives of the causal world if we are pure. The initiates used to portray Saturn as a skeleton and the skeleton symbolizes all that is most durable. Everything else may die and wither away, but the bones remain. The physical, astral and mental bodies die but the causal body is immortal.

As long as you have a skeleton, some bones, you can put flesh on them and breathe life into them. There is a passage in the Old Testament which tells of how the Almighty, having carried off the Prophet Ezekiel and set him down in a valley full of dry bones, said to him, *'Prophesy to these bones, and say to them, "O dry bones, hear the word of the Lord! Thus says the Lord God to these bones: 'I will cause breath to enter you and you shall live. I shall put sinews on you and bring flesh upon you, cover you with skin and put breath in you; and you shall live. Then you shall know that I am the Lord.'"'* The same idea is present in the twentieth card of the Tarot, the Judgement, which shows an angel blowing a blast on a trumpet and awakening the dead. There are some great mysteries contained in this card which corresponds to certain events in the life of a disciple as well as in the life of humanity as a whole. And the Gospels tell us that Christ said, *'Do not be astonished at this; for the hour is coming when all who are in their graves will hear his voice and will come out.'*

Everywhere, throughout the world, now, the initiates are telling us, 'Wake up, the sun is already rising over the earth. It is pouring out its light and warmth on us. Unite with all men in a spirit of love and light. Darkness is disappearing; the new life is beginning. Come and work with us and we shall show you the treasures of life.' But, as I have already said, beings of a higher order speak only briefly and very softly within us. They murmur, 'Be watchful. Love. Study. Ally yourselves with heaven. Be pure. Open your hearts to the Lord. Be at peace.' Whereas others never stop talking and insisting, night and day, always ready with all kinds of arguments to persuade us to do what they want us to do. It is possible to hear and understand the voice of higher beings speaking to us in our hearts, but only if their voices speak in the midst of a profound silence. This is why initiates fast frequently: in order to create silence within themselves. When one eats to the point of being surfeited, one stirs up a great commotion within, for all one's animals start clamouring and shouting for their share of the food. Whereas the most extraordinary sense of peace takes hold of one who fasts, and it is only in the midst of this peace that the voice of God can be heard.

Henceforth we must learn to be friends with Saturn. As long as we have not learned to love Saturn, the relationship between us will be strained. Whereas, once we love him, that is to say: once we love wisdom, silence, meditation and perseverance, Saturn will be kind to us. Saturn represents a system identical to our own solar system with planets comparable to Mars, Jupiter, the Earth and the Moon, etc. This means that there is a copy of our planet Earth and of all that it includes, in his system, and each one of us has our double on the Saturnian earth. Saturn observes everything that happens: he sees everything, knows everything, takes note of everything. Whether you are unjust, dishonest and malicious and refuse to obey the divine law or whether, on the contrary, you are trying to grow in perfection and to become wiser and more indulgent, Saturn immediately knows it and inscribes it in the lines of your hand.

And now I want to tell you one more thing. Certain initiates know how to prepare a liquid which they call the 'universal spirit' and which they extract from the atmosphere and from snow, rain and dew. It is a condensation of the spirit of nature which animates all things.[7] If you possess some of this liquid you can find out how a friend is by putting a drop of his blood into a small quantity of it; if your friend is well, this figure ⊙, like a cell with its nucleus, will be formed in the liquid. If he is resting, the liquid will show no change except a very slight darkening. If he is ill, there will be no light in the drop of blood, and if he dies during the experiment, the flask of liquid will shatter. Saturn, like this 'universal spirit', has the power to see and understand the state of all things. This is why it is Saturn who rewards and punishes: he represents destiny.* But it is in our power to change

* In this context, it is interesting to note that contemporary studies in anatomy and nuclear physics both confirm Initiatic Science. The Master Omraam Mikhaël Aïvanhov often talked about the Sephirotic Tree of Life of the Cabbalah which, he thought, was the system which best explained and depicted the structure of the universe. And, in the Tree of Life, the planet Saturn, which the Master associates with the ears, resides in the sephirah Binah in which the Twenty-four Elders preside over the destiny of all created beings. Binah is the sephirah that represents stability and lead is its corresponding metal.

A first element which confirms these correspondences is the number twenty-four which is found in two separate instances in the structure of the ear: first in the length of the auditory canal (24 millimetres) and, secondly, in the 24,000 rods of the organ of Corti, the essential auditory organ. On the other hand, physicists speak of three series of natural radioactive elements, of which the first element in each series, actinium, thorium and uranium, decays through a succession of radioactive substances and ends its life as a non-radioactive isotope of lead. Is it not striking that all three series of naturally radioactive substances should reach the same ultimate end, as an isotope of the stable element lead? There is certainly good reason to see lead as a symbol of stability, and it seems quite likely that other, similar confirmations may well exist in this domain. (Editor's note) our destiny if we know how to distinguish good things from bad, if we can hear the difference between the voice of higher beings and that of inferior beings, if we know how to maintain ourselves in a state of spiritual equilibrium.

Today I received a magnificent formula from my Master, and I would like to share it with you. In Bulgaria, the whole Brotherhood recites it twice a day, at 8 o'clock, morning and evening. It is an excellent formula which can be a bond to link us to the White Brotherhood. Here it is:

'I will live by the rule of love, exactly as we have been taught by Christ; may my life improve with love! I will live by the law of God; may my life be transformed in accordance with God's wish.'

Let us live with love and wisdom. Let us be kind and patient; let us open our hearts and souls to the love that comes to warm and vivify us each day. Let us open our minds and spirits to the wisdom that comes to illuminate and enlighten us and guide us on the path of truth! If we are children of light, we shall be healthy, happy, beautiful and powerful: images of the living God. Amen. So may it be!

Paris, 19 February 1938

Notes
1. See *'In Spirit and in Truth'*, Izvor Coll. n° 235, chap. 9: 'The Skin'.
2. See *Les deux arbres du Paradis,* Complete Works, vol. 3, chap. 3: 'Ce que révèle le visage humain'.
3. See *'Know Thyself'–Jnana Yoga,* Complete Works, vol. 18, chap. 3: 'The Power of Thought'.
4. See *The Philosopher's Stone – in the Gospels and in Alchemy,* Izvor Coll. n° 241, chap. 2: 'It is not what goes into the mouth that defiles a person...'

5. See *The Path of Silence,* Izvor Coll. n° 229, chap. 12: 'The Voice of Silence is the Voice of God'.
6. See *Man's Two Natures, Human and Divine,* Izvor Coll. n° 213, chap. 8: 'The Silent Voice of the Higher Self' and *The Path of Silence,* Izvor Coll. n° 229, chap. 14: 'A Silent Room'.
7. See *The Philosopher's Stone – in the Gospels and in Alchemy,* Izvor Coll. n° 241, chap. 12: 'The May dew'.

Chapter Five

LOVE IS HIDDEN IN THE MOUTH

'"Very truly, I tell you, whoever believes has eternal life. I am the bread of life. Your ancestors ate the manna in the wilderness, and they died. This is the bread that comes down from heaven, so that one may eat of it and not die. I am the living bread that came down from heaven. Whoever eats of this bread will live for ever; and the bread that I will give for the life of the world is my flesh."

The Jews then disputed among themselves, saying, "How can this man give us his flesh to eat?" So Jesus said to them, "Very truly, I tell you, unless you eat the flesh of the Son of Man and drink his blood, you have no life in you. Those who eat my flesh and drink my blood have eternal life, and I will raise them up on the last day; for my flesh is true food and my blood is true drink. Those who eat my flesh and drink my blood abide in me, and I in them. Just as the living Father sent me, and I live because of the Father, so whoever eats me will live because of me."'

John 6, 47-57

'Those who eat my flesh and drink my blood have eternal life'. To eat the flesh of Christ and to drink his blood... We must obviously understand these words in their symbolical sense and try to interpret their meaning.

The flesh and blood of Christ are the bread and wine; the bread made from wheat and the wine made from grapes. Bread is the flesh and wine, the blood. The symbols of bread and wine are to be found in all Initiations.

You have certainly read the account in *Genesis* of how Abraham met the high priest of the living God, Melchizedek, king of Salem: *'And the king of Sodom went out to meet him at the Valley of Shaveh (that is, the King's Valley), after his return from the defeat of Chedorlaomer and the kings who were with him. Then Melchizedek king of Salem brought out bread and wine; he was the priest of God Most High. And he blessed him and said: "Blessed be Abram by God Most High, maker of heaven and earth; and blessed be God Most High, who has delivered your enemies into your hand." And Abram gave him one-tenth of everything.'*

The name Melchizedek, which means 'king of righteousness' is formed from two Hebrew words: *melek,* meaning 'king' and *tsedek,* which means 'righteousness', and the name of the city of which he was king, Salem, comes from the same root as the word *shalom,* meaning 'peace'. Melchizedek, therefore, is the king of justice and peace, but we don't know much more than that about him; he is a very mysterious being. Only the great Initiates know something about him and there is only one other passage in the Bible that speaks of him, and that is in St Paul's *Letter to the Hebrews.* St Paul writes: *"This 'King Melchizedek of Salem, priest of the Most High God, met Abraham as he was returning from defeating the kings and blessed him'; and to him Abraham apportioned 'one-tenth of everything'. His name, in the first place, means 'king of righteousness'; next he is also king of Salem, that is, 'king of peace'. Without father, without mother, without genealogy, having neither beginning of days nor end of life, but resembling the Son of God, he remains a priest for ever. See how great he is! Even Abraham the patriarch gave him a tenth of the spoils. "* I shall talk to you about Melchizedek another time.

The Lord's Supper instituted by Jesus was a repetition of the gift of bread and wine that Melchizedek made to Abraham. In fact, St Paul also says that Jesus was *'a priest for ever, according to the order of Melchizedek.'*[1] The legend of the Holy Grail is also related to the mystery of bread and wine... But, interesting though these questions may be, that is not what I want to talk about today.

The wheat growing in the fields and the grapes in the vineyard are symbols of the two principles, masculine and feminine, which are to be found in all Initiations; that is to say, symbols of wisdom and love. The vine is the heart, the wine the blood, that is to say, the feelings. Whereas the field is the head, the intellect, and the wheat represents thoughts. This means that if we eat the wisdom that grows from the spirit and drink the love which flows from the heart, we shall have eternal life. It is only by means of wisdom and love that man can win eternal life.

We eat and drink and, in doing so, we use our mouths. Everyone has a mouth, and with what wisdom nature has designed it, how many secrets it contains! In the preceding lectures I told you that man represented a triangle, the three sides of which are the mind, the heart and the will. I also said that the ideal of the mind was divine wisdom, that of the heart divine love and that of the will divine freedom. And we saw that this triangle was present everywhere, in every domain of nature. I explained that the eyes represented truth and the ears wisdom, and now, this evening, I shall talk to you about the mouth which represents love. Perhaps you would also like to know what the nose represents? Well, for the moment, it is enough for you to know that it represents the whole man. It is something in the nature of a manometer which indicates the pressure of a liquid. It enables one to gauge the intensity of a person's inner light and to see how his energies are distributed. It is made up of three parts... But I shall talk to you about that another time.

So, this evening, we shall study the mouth, which represents man's feelings, emotions, passions and instincts. The mouth, as you know, is part of the digestive system; it is by means of our mouths that we eat and drink. Astrologically it is connected to

Venus (the planet of love) and to Mercury, because of the tongue which is so skilful in both good and evil. The mouth, together with the tongue, therefore, represents a partnership between Venus and Mercury, in one of their manifestations in the world. The tongue is Mercury, the god who metamorphoses, Hermes, the messenger of the gods who appears successively in the guise of Saturn, Mars, Uranus or the Moon.

The mouth is the seat both of taste and of the word, and the tongue is active and proficient in both these functions. The tongue, it is said, has no bone but it is capable of breaking bones; it has no rope but it is capable of putting the hangman's noose round a man's neck; it has no sword, but it is capable of piercing hearts!

On the upper surface of the tongue we find the taste buds, and on the lower surface, the salivary glands.

As I have already told you, anyone who wants to study the occult sciences, should begin by studying his own physical body, because all the sciences are contained in man. He who wants to study alchemy, therefore, should first study it in himself, in the mouth and its functions and in the food that it absorbs each day, because that food contains all chemical and alchemical elements.

The astrological signs that correspond to the planet Venus are Taurus and Libra (♉ ♎). The mouth, therefore, is related to Taurus, the throat (as you see, this symbol resembles a tongue), and to Libra, the kidneys. The signs that correspond to Mercury are Gemini and Virgo (♊ ♍); Gemini is linked to the arms and Virgo to the solar plexus and intestines. In ancient times, Mercury was reputed to be the ingenious, skilful god who could do everything; he was Hermes the magician who healed and worked miracles with his *caduceus,*[2] the magic wand with its two, intertwined serpents representing the two hands. From the esoteric point of view, the two serpents are the two currents that traverse the universe: love and hatred, attraction and repulsion, life and death, electricity and magnetism, heat and cold, light and darkness, and all magic is based on a knowledge of these two currents. An initiate heals and works miracles with his hands which represent two coiled snakes.

The energies channelled through the hands flow from the solar plexus. Knowing this, you can see how Mercury's two houses, Gemini and Virgo, are related to each other.

Whatever we eat and drink has to be processed by the kidneys, and if we eat and drink unwisely and overload the kidneys, they cannot eliminate the waste products efficiently and this leads to various anomalies such as kidney stones or gravel, and so on. A kidney is another kind of liver; like the liver, it purifies the blood and absorbs poisons; the kidneys are a factory for the production of urine, a poison which then has to be evacuated. Just as it is possible to determine the state of a person's health by looking at his tongue, his general condition can also be determined by analysis of his urine. I have not got time, this evening, to show you how the astrological symbols can explain the account in *Genesis* of the fall of man. The zodiacal sign opposite to Taurus (which represents the mouth and throat) is Scorpio. And Scorpio is the serpent spoken of in *Genesis,* the astrological sign that corresponds to the sexual organs.[3]

We have already seen that the organ of equilibrium, the cluster of three semicircular canals, is situated in the ears. The kidneys also constitute a centre of equilibrium, for their function is to ensure the stability of the composition of the blood; also, they are placed exactly half-way up the physical body. Astrologically, the kidneys are associated with Libra, symbol of balance or equilibrium, and the ears, too, are related to Libra, since they are ruled by Saturn which is exalted in Libra. Still another link between the ears and the kidneys is provided by the grains of calcareous matter found in the endolymphatic fluid: in the ears, these particles are in their proper place and serve a useful purpose in helping to maintain physical balance; in the kidneys, however, grains of calcareous matter can become stones and cause very serious health problems.

   When we studied the triangle formed by the three principles of mind, heart and will in relation to colours, we saw that yellow corresponded to the brain, blue to the lungs and red to the stomach. But each colour is also related to its complementary colour on the six-pointed star: red is related to green, blue to orange and yellow to violet (Figure 31).

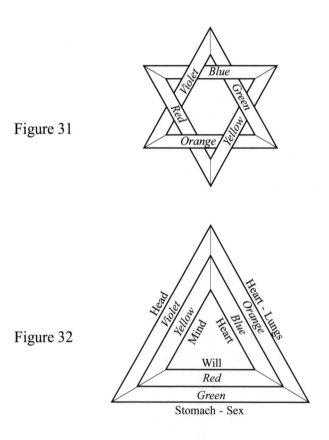

Figure 31

Figure 32

   Red and green work on the level of the stomach and sexual organs; red in the manifestation of vitality and green in the digestive process. Blue and orange work in the lungs and heart;

orange signifies the health born of respiration and blue represents peace. Yellow and violet work in the head; yellow is the colour of the intellect, of wisdom, and violet is the colour of mystical sentiment, adoration of the Creator (See Figure 32).

And now let's look at the world of plants. On the under-side of the leaves of plants are thousands of minute openings called stomata which are like tiny mouths through which leaves absorb and evacuate gases and water vapour. A plant breathes, perspires and assimilates through its stomata. Assimilation consists in the decomposition of carbon dioxide from the atmosphere into carbon and oxygen; the carbon serves as nourishment for the plant, and the oxygen is released into the air. Assimilation is effected by the action of light on the three pigments contained in leaves: xanthophyll, carotene and chlorophyll.

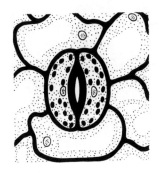

Figure 33   A stoma

Xanthophyll is yellow, carotene is a reddish orange and chlorophyll is green and, since the complementary colours of yellow, orange and green are violet, blue and red, we find, once again, the triangle we were talking about a moment ago (Figure 32).

There are at least three circumstances in life in which human beings are in complete understanding: when they are gathered round the table to eat together, when they sing together and when they pray together. And this brings us back again, as you see, to the triangle of six colours, and we can complete the picture with the following table:

Red – Green   Chlorophyll   Nutrition
Blue – Orange   Carotene   Song
Yellow – Violet   Xanthophyll   Prayer and contemplation

You have certainly noticed that men do exactly the reverse of plants, that is to say, they breathe in the gas released by plants and expel that which plants breathe in and assimilate. The head of plants is below, for their head is their roots, the organ of nutrition, whereas their sexual organs are their flowers, the organs of reproduction. If you look at a tree you cannot see its head; you only see its leaves, which are its lungs; its head (the roots) is underground.

And now, let's get back to the mouth and look at the taste buds and the salivary glands. The taste buds, with their nerve fibres and sensitive cilia, resemble ears of wheat, whereas the salivary glands resemble bunches of grapes (Figure 34).

Figure 34

Taste bud   Salivary gland

What is extremely striking is that Mercury and Venus, both of which influence the mouth, are connected, on the one hand (Mercury), with the constellation of Virgo, portrayed as a young woman holding a sheaf of wheat, symbol of the harvests of the month of August, and, on the other (Venus), with the constellation of Libra which corresponds to September and October, the months of the grape harvest. The months of wheat (August) and of wine (September) come next to each other, and they are the months of Mercury and Venus.

Jesus said, *'Those who eat my flesh and drink my blood have eternal life.'* How can we eat this flesh and drink this blood? It is in the mouth that we find the answer to this question. Wisdom (the flesh of Christ), is related to the symbol of wheat, the sense of taste, therefore: the taste buds. Love (the blood of Christ), is related to grapes and, therefore, to the salivary glands. To be wise is to taste, and to love is to secrete juices. The salivary glands secrete saliva, and saliva contains enzymes which, in exactly the same way as chlorophyll, carotene and xanthophyll, act on the food we eat to transform it. If you eat automatically, with no awareness of what you are doing, without love or gratitude, or if you entertain negative feelings of anger or discontent while you are eating, the secretions of your salivary glands will be affected, for there is a connection between your thoughts and feelings and these glands and, when they are negatively affected, your saliva is diluted with elements which are powerless to transform your food. In the long run, this leads to problems in the stomach or the digestive tract. The tongue has been put in the mouth to serve as a kind of customs officer; it tastes and sorts out what you put in your mouth. If the customs officer is absent or corrupt, all kinds of harmful elements can slip through customs!

It is important to know that if we absorb our food without thinking about it or loving it, we only absorb its crudest physical components, and these cannot contribute to the construction of our spiritual being; whereas, if we eat with great love and in full awareness of what we are doing, our salivary glands secrete substances which transform these physical elements and make them immediately absorbable. Food contains very subtle elements, comparable to our own souls and spirits, but if we eat in a state of fear, anger or frustration, we cannot absorb them, and that is a pity. This is why, when I eat, I prefer to do so in silence, so that I can think about the nutrients that I am going to absorb. You will object that our thoughts cannot possibly change the functioning of our glands, and to that I must answer that all our thoughts as well the pictures in our imagination and anything that affects us in any way, also directly affects our glands. If I slice a lemon and start eating it in front of you, you will immediately feel your salivary glands beginning to secrete their juices; even the mention of this is sufficient to trigger the reaction!

Some people experience others as a flavour. Jesus said, *'You will know them by their fruits.'* Some people are sweet, others are salty, others sour... And astrologers see a correspondence between the different flavours and the planets: bitterness corresponds to Saturn, pepperiness to Mars, insipidity to the Moon, sweetness to Venus, saltiness to the Sun and sourness to Mercury. Yes, you can know men from their fruits. He who is lacking in red and green will not produce good fruits on the physical plane; he who lacks blue and orange will not produce good fruits on the astral plane, and he who lacks yellow and violet will not produce good fruits on the mental plane. But he who possesses all the colours will produce good fruits on every plane.

A moment ago, I mentioned the power of thought, and I would like to say a few words about this. In certain underground stations or subways, the escalators are set in motion by a photoelectric cell. When someone steps in front of the source of light, it triggers a reaction in the receiver cell which sets the mechanism of the staircase in motion. And this is an image of how everything functions in nature, in which the sun triggers a series of reactions in plants, animals and human beings. In the future, human beings will use the sun's rays for all their realizations; all other sources of energy will be exhausted and men will have to get their energy from the only inexhaustible source, the sun. Initiates have always used the sun's rays, but the rays they use are the hidden, invisible rays, the virtues; he who possesses the virtues possesses all the rays. A time is coming, however, when everyone will learn to use the sun to heal themselves and even to work towards their own perfection, to become honest, noble and luminous.

The works of nature are so marvellously put together. When we think, our thoughts are like beams of light which traverse our being; if they are evil, the beam is deflected and triggers the mechanism of a moving staircase which carries our consciousness down to hell. But if they are upright and just, the same escalators carry us upwards. Anyone who thinks he can hoodwink nature is deceiving himself; it is not possible. Nobody has ever yet succeeded in outwitting nature. Nature is infinitely wiser than men; she has thousands of years of experience behind her and it is she who has designed things in such a way that the effects of the forces that act upon us depend on the nature of our own thoughts, feelings and actions. Our 'factory' is equipped with certain instruments about which we still know very little and, when we entertain perverse thoughts or feelings, these instruments are automatically set in motion and our glands begin to secrete poisonous substances... And then we wonder why we have a pain in our stomach, head or chest. These pains are nature's way of speaking to us. They are her way of saying, 'Why did you take this path? It is your own fault if you have to suffer: you stretched out your hand to pluck forbidden fruit, and it was this that triggered the alarm!'

If we eat with love, our glands secrete substances which have a favourable effect on our food and it starts to be transformed even before it has left our mouth. The stomach is simply a repetition on another level of the cavity formed by the mouth; the mouth is a small spiritual stomach. You are wondering how the mouth can be a spiritual stomach; let me tell you. Suppose you have been fasting for three days and are feeling faint with hunger. You take some fruit and begin to eat; immediately, even before you have digested or assimilated anything, you begin to feel your strength coming back. Where does that strength come from? This spiritual assimilation is something that everyone experiences, but to a different degree. Every human being eats, but labourers, scientists, poets, criminals, idlers and initiates all eat very differently. Observe the way in which you eat and you will understand a great deal about yourself. One could almost say, 'Show me how you eat and I'll tell you who you are.'

If we learn to eat according to initiatic rules, we can become highly skilled alchemists. The alchemists used to look for the philosophers' stone which would transform metals into gold.[4] Yes, but an alchemist must be more than a good chemist. A chemist only needs material elements for his experiments, but an alchemist has to include non-material elements in his formulas. In fact, this is why some alchemists who knew the formula for the philosophers' stone by heart and made all their preparations with the utmost care, still failed to get the results they hoped for. They were not good, true alchemists. A true alchemist knows that he not only has to prepare the chemical ingredients strictly according to the formula, he must also contribute a spiritual ingredient in the form of a force emanating from himself, for this alone can set in motion the alchemical process. Many people know a great many secrets intellectually, but they get no results because they possess neither the necessary power nor the necessary virtues. To produce the philosophers' stone is less a physical than a psychic and spiritual process. He who wishes to obtain the philosophers' stone must take care to study the virtues and acquire them inwardly; only if he does this will matter obey him. This is why those who use no discrimination either in their choice of food or in the way they eat, who are unaware of what they are doing and devoid of love and gratitude towards their food or towards him who provides it... this is why such men may be good chemists, but they will never be good alchemists. Whereas he who eats with love and awareness transforms the process and his food becomes pure gold.

You will ask, 'Why don't you talk to us about the great mysteries? About the angels and archangels and the higher worlds?'[5] I will talk to you about all that, one day, but if you don't know how to eat consciously and with love, even the greatest mysteries will be of no use to you. You have to learn how to eat, at the same time, in all three worlds: physical, astral and mental. If we don't know how to eat, the angels and archangels will close the doors of their kingdom to us and tell us: 'What have you come here for? Go away! Go and learn how to eat before coming here!' You will object that you don't need to eat in order to be well informed. True, but you may know all about the peel of an orange; you will never learn to enjoy its juice.

I have already talked to you about fasting. Today I want to add something to what I said before. If you never fast, your cells become lazy; they get out of the habit of working as they should and the tubes and ducts of your body begin to be clogged up. Whereas, if you fast, your cells say to each other, 'What's happening? Our master is letting us die...' and they bestir themselves and start working properly again. When they see that you are not giving them anything to eat, they begin to realize that if they do nothing about it they will die, so the lungs begin to breathe deeply in order to absorb etheric nourishment from the atmosphere. This is why fasting is so useful. I have often verified this for myself (In fact, when I talk to you about something, it is never because I have learned it from books. Everything I tell you comes from centuries of personal experience). When you go without eating for two or three days, your cells become stronger and better able to absorb nutrients from the atmosphere which are subtler than physical nutrients. Similarly, if you hold your breath for a moment or two, your thought begins to work on a higher plane. This is why initiates have developed methods for holding their breath in order to release the powers lying dormant in the brain. When they fast, their respiration becomes more powerful, and when they hold their breath, their thought becomes more powerful. In fact, they also know how to arrest all thought processes, thereby intensifying the action of the spirit within them.

If one always eats one's fill, one ends by becoming short of breath because one's respiratory capacity decreases... and one's capacity for reflection even more so! When one fasts, on the other hand, breathing becomes easier, one's circulation improves and one's whole being is flooded with peace. If you practise holding your breath you can learn to project very powerful thoughts into space. One day, if you like, I will talk to you about how thoughts travel through space.[6]

The mouth reveals many very important things. It tells us, for instance, that we must love and establish a relationship of mutual exchange with nature. Jesus said, *'You are the salt of the earth; but if salt has lost its taste, how can its saltiness be restored? It is no longer good for anything, but is thrown out and trampled underfoot.'*[7] Salt is the child of its father and mother, acid and alkali. Jesus' words mean, 'You are the salt, that is to say the truth, because truth is the child of wisdom (the father) and love (the mother). If you lose your flavour, in other words, if you cease to eat wisdom and drink love, you will be thrown away, because you will have lost your power. You must always be full of love and wisdom in order to possess warmth and light.'

Perhaps you are thinking that, although I keep talking to you about love, you don't really know how to love. That is true; men don't know how to love. They did know, once, but now they have forgotten. There was a time when men knew how to love, how to think and also how to unravel the mysteries of nature, but they have lost the light of this knowledge. Every time a man sins or commits a crime, he extinguishes one of his inner lamps, and now he no longer has the light he needs to read the book of living nature, he no longer knows how to love! And yet it is so easy to love... but no one is willing to make an effort.

I once had a friend in Bulgaria who was very rich but always unhappy. One day, I met him in the street and he said, 'You look as though you were bursting with joy; what have you been doing?' 'Oh, nothing much', I replied; 'I've just bought some joy.' 'You're joking', he answered; 'How can you buy joy?' 'No, no, I'm not joking; it's perfectly true: I have just bought some joy, and it didn't even cost much!' 'Tell me how you did it', said my friend; 'I have spent a great deal of money in my life but I have never experienced joy.' He was looking at me with an expression of disbelief and astonishment, and yet he knew me well and he knew that I wouldn't deceive him. So I said, 'Come with me; I'll show you... Look; there's a man who sells joy.' We were looking at a poor old man who had a tray of buttons, shoe-laces and string for sale. 'Yes, look at him', I said; 'A long time ago that man was a great initiate, but he made a lot of mistakes and now he has to stand there, in all weathers, waiting for people to buy his wares. Go and take something from his tray, some boot-laces, for instance, and ask him how much they are. He will tell you, "Ten levs." Then you can give him fifty and tell him to keep the change. He will be amazed and very happy. He will think, "Ah, there are still some kind people in the world." His faith will be strengthened, and you will share his joy; you will feel it vibrating within you all day long... and it will have cost you only a few pennies.' My friend understood what I was saying and was delighted. Then I added, 'You can go and see someone who is ill, also. Take them a small gift of some kind and say a few kind words. Tell them that God is merciful and everything will turn out all right. When you try to comfort others and give them a little joy, you too will know joy. But you must be careful to choose the right person to visit, because not everybody can accept joy.' Obviously, there are a great many other ways of finding joy.[8]

There is not very much time left, this evening, but I still want to say something about the magical power of words.

There are two categories of magicians: those who practise magic by nothing but the power of words, and those who do so with the help of an instrument of some kind, usually a wand.

The former are the more highly evolved, because their magic instrument is an intrinsic part of themselves: their tongue; whereas others need to hold a wand, and the wand, of course, is never actually part of themselves. The *caduceus* belonged to Mercury, the god of magic, and Mercury rules both the tongue and the hands. You are familiar with the beginning of St John's Gospel: *'In the beginning was the Word, and the Word was with God, and the Word was God. He was in the beginning with God. All things came into being through him, and without him not one thing came into being.'* [9] And man too, in the beginning, knew how to create through the power of the Word; it was only gradually, as he became more and more deeply immersed in matter, that he lost the power of the Word and was obliged to use his hands in order to create. In the beginning, men were kings; they had only to give an order and whatever they wanted was immediately accomplished, for kings always have servants at their beck and call to carry out their orders. Later, men fell from their kingly state to a state of subordination and slavery and, as a result, could no longer act by means of their mouth; they had to use their hands. And, today, mankind is obliged to work with matter so as to fashion it and draw subsistence from it according to God's words to Adam: *'By the sweat of your face you shall eat bread.'* Before the Fall, man had servants who did whatever he commanded; this is why it is said that he dwelt in paradise, for toil and suffering are unknown in paradise. Those who refuse to do the will of God will be placed in circumstances where they have to earn their living in the midst of difficulties.

The world was created by the Word. A science exists that teaches us how to speak, that is to say, how to speak to those who dwell within us, for our subjects, our children, are within us, not outside us. We all want to teach others and give them orders, but this is very difficult. We have to begin by teaching our own cells; it is to them that we should give orders. Sages don't say very much out loud because they are in the habit of speaking to those who dwell within them. But observe yourselves: if you talk to someone, in your imagination, you will notice that your tongue moves in your mouth; it moves according to what you are thinking. Why? Because thoughts are linked to words and your tongue reproduces the movement of your thoughts although, of course, if you are not actually speaking out loud, it does so on a very reduced scale. And this is what magic consists of. Our tongue is linked to our thoughts more intimately than any other part of our bodies; this is why it provides such a good example of how thoughts can influence our cells. The tongue, which follows the movement of our reflections, proves that all the other cells of our bodies are also set in motion, harmoniously or otherwise, depending on the nature of our thoughts. You will say that there is no visible proof of this... Perhaps not, but on the subtle planes there is an imperceptible movement, the effects of which will become evident in the future.

The hands are related to Gemini and the solar plexus to Virgo, and Mercury is the ruler of both these signs. It is Mercury, therefore, who rules the hands as well as the solar plexus and the tongue. Bend your right arm and put your hand on your solar plexus and you will have a triangle formed by your mouth, your elbow and your solar plexus. If you keep your arm in this position as you speak to your cells, they will listen to you, because the solar plexus controls all the cells and all the unconscious functions of the body: growth, secretions, circulation, digestion, elimination, respiration, etc.[10] This is how we can speak to our cells and get them to listen to us, and all the more so, if our faith and our power of concentration is very great. We can also speak to other human beings and to the intelligent forces of nature by means of our hands.

If I talk to you in this way, it is because I have experimented and verified the truth of everything I tell you, for years, and because I want to help you. This evening I have been like nourishment to you, and you have been like mouths absorbing this nourishment. But if the words you hear are not received with love, they will be no use to you. If you listen with closed minds or an attitude of criticism and cynicism, if you think that what I say is nonsense, you will be incapable of assimilating the nourishment I am giving you and it will have no effect on you.

To know how to eat represents an immense, profound science, and it is sad to see that so many supposedly intelligent and well educated people know nothing about this, and continue to feed like animals. I would have liked to reveal to you, this evening, the tremendous breadth and depth of the secrets contained in food. What I have told you about the Lord's Supper is nothing compared to what it is in reality: this mystery contains all the secrets of communion.[11] For communion is to be in touch, every day, at every hour of the day and with every fibre of one's being, with the living forces of nature: stones, plants, mountains, springs, the sun, the stars and, above all, with all living creatures. But who ever thinks about that? People are content to go to church from time to time and communicate by means of the bread and wine; they think that that is sufficient. No, it is not enough; he who knows how to communicate is capable of being in touch, by means of his love and wisdom, with all human beings, with their souls and spirits. Only when we truly understand this question of communion shall we be able to say that we eat the flesh of Christ and drink His blood; only then will all our cells and every level of our being be flooded with true life, with pure, abundant, noble life, the everlasting life that has neither beginning nor end.

My wish for you is that you will always be linked to love and wisdom for, when you eat divine wisdom and drink divine love, you will have eternal life.

Paris, 26 February 1938

Notes
1. See *Sons and Daughters of God,* Izvor Coll. n° 240, chap. 6: 'Jesus, Priest of the Most High according to the Order of Melchizedek'.

2. See *Cosmic Balance – The Secret of Polarity,* Izvor Coll. n° 237, chap. 9: 'The Caduceus of Hermes – The Astral Serpent', and *Light is a Living Spirit,* Izvor Coll. n° 212, chap. 9: 'The Spiritual Laser'.
3. See *Les deux arbres du Paradis,* Complete Works, vol. 3, chap. 9: 'Les deux arbres du Paradis: 1. Les axes Bélier-Balance et Taureau-Scorpion – 2. Le serpent de la Genèse'.
4. See *The Philosopher's Stone – in the Gospels and in Alchemy,* Izvor Coll. n° 241, chap. 10: 'The philosopher's stone, fruit of a mystic union'.
5. See *The Fruits of The Tree of Life – The Cabbalistic Tradition,* Complete Works, vol. 32, and *Angels and other Mysteries of The Tree of Life,* Izvor Coll. n° 236.
6. See *The Powers of Thought,* Izvor Coll. n° 224, chap. 4: 'Thoughts are Living Beings'.
7. See *The Philosopher's Stone – in the Gospels and in Alchemy,* Izvor Coll. n° 241, chap. 3: 'You are the salt of the earth', and chap. 4: 'But if the salt loses its flavour…'.
8. See *The Wellsprings of Eternal Joy,* Izvor Coll. n° 242.
9. See *'Au commencement était le Verbe' – commentaires des Évangiles,* Complete Works, vol. 9, chap. 1: 'Au commencement était le Verbe…'.
10. See *Man's Subtle Bodies and Centres – the Aura, the Solar Plexus, the Chakras…,* Izvor Coll. n° 219, chap. 3: 'The Solar Plexus'.
11. See *The Yoga of Nutrition,* Izvor Coll. n° 204, chap. 8: 'Communion'.

Chapter Six

LOVE, WISDOM AND TRUTH
(Mouth, ears and eyes)

This evening I want to say something more about the eyes, the ears and the mouth. No doubt you will be thinking that I have already told you quite enough about them? Yes, but there are still a great many interesting things to say about these organs.

Every day, you eat bread, drink water or wine and breathe air, and you never really tire of all that food. Well, when we are here together, I am your cook: I have already given you liquid nourishment for your mouth, aerial nourishment for your ears and etheric nourishment for your eyes. And what is on the menu this evening? This evening the menu calls for a mixture of all three kinds of food: liquid, aerial and etheric. One after the other I have revealed to you the three letters A, U and M, and now we are going to combine these three sounds to make the word Aum.

A is for your eyes
U is for your ears
M is for your mouth.

In an earlier lecture I talked about the passage in the Gospel which says, *'Ask, and it will be given to you; search, and you will find; knock, and the door will be opened for you.'* At first sight, these precepts seem to be very simple. 'Ask', for instance... is there anything we don't ask for? We all have families, friends and lovers and we never stop asking God and the invisible world, nature and the angels, for everything they could possibly need or wish for. But then, when we don't get what we have asked for, we are disappointed and conclude that the invisible world is treating us unjustly. We have so often asked to no avail. Why? Simply because we are ignorant of the laws involved. When you see something in a shop that you want to buy, you ask a salesman for it, that is true, but that is not the end of it: you also have to give something in exchange. If you refuse to pay, you will not be given anything at all. In nature, in the invisible world, the system is exactly the same as in the shops of the physical world. The invisible world tells us, 'Give your heart to God and he will give you everything in exchange.' But you reply, 'I can't; I've already given it to others... I have a wife and children, and an adorable mistress: I have no heart left to give.' This is why your prayers are never answered. You imagine that you are going to be able to get something for nothing; but it is impossible. *'Ask, and it will be given to you'* implies, first and foremost, that you give something. You have to give part of your conscious attention, part of your time and your daily efforts, part of your thoughts and feelings. If you do that, then you will receive.

'Search, and you will find.' Jesus also said, *'Walk while you have the light, so that the darkness may not overtake you. If you walk in the darkness, you do not know where you are going.'* So we have to seek while it is still light. A great many scientists and philosophers seek God very sincerely, but they do so at night. They want to see the sun, but they look for it after it has set... so how can they? And then, because they have been looking for it in the dark, they conclude that it does not exist and publish the results of their research, claiming that forty or fifty years of rigorously scientific observation has forced them to conclude that there is no such thing as the sun; even on their death-beds, they say that they have never found the sun. At the heart of contemporary culture is

a research that has been conducted in the dark. Even men's daily lives are organized so that most of their activities take place at night. But what I am saying applies particularly to the symbolic aspect: if, after years of research, a man has failed to find the sun (that is to say, the meaning of life), it means that he has led a nocturnal existence and been going to bed in the morning, just when it was time for the sun to rise, so as not to see it.

'Knock, and the door will be opened for you.' This precept is connected with the ears. You are familiar with the structure of the ear. Sounds enter through the auditory canal and are communicated to the inner ear by means of the ear-drum and the three small bones (hammer, anvil and stirrup). If the frequency of a sound is too low (infrasonic) or too high (supersonic), we hear nothing.

I would like to help you to understand how wonderfully everything in nature is designed. The organ of Corti is built like a musical instrument, with a series of cords of different lengths, each of which resonates in response to sounds having the same vibrational frequency. In every area of the universe, every being and every object resonates in response to vibrations of the same frequency as its own. This is why, when we emit on low frequencies, we get back the same low frequencies. If we want God to hear our messages, we have to emit on very high frequencies, in other words, our thoughts and feelings must be very pure, noble and disinterested. If we emit waves of hatred, jealousy or anger, for instance, God will not hear us, but other creatures will, and we shall receive similar messages from them in response.

People have often said to me, 'I have asked the invisible world for many things, but I never get any of the things I wanted', or, 'I have prayed to the Lord, but I don't know if he'll answer me.' In other words, 'I have knocked, but I have no idea if anyone is going to open to me.' So then I ask them, 'What did you pray for?' One tells me that he prayed for wealth, another for fame, another for a pretty wife, etc. In that case, of course, you may have to wait a very long time before getting what you asked for,

because the administrative services on high are swamped by so
many requests of this kind that they have a very heavy backlog.

Everyone clamours for money, women, pleasure, power and
privilege. If that is the kind of thing you are asking for, you
may well have to wait for another incarnation before getting it.
You will ask, 'Well, what should we be asking for?' Ask and
knock in order to get what nobody else thinks of asking for.
Everybody competes for the same goods of this world; they all
rush off in pursuit of material goods, and the invisible world is
snowed under with their covetous demands. Of course, this is all
symbolic because, in reality, whatever you ask for, the invisible
world is perfectly capable of giving it to you instantly, if it wants
to. But even so, I strongly advise you, instead of always looking
for material satisfactions, to ask for the light, love and wisdom
that will enable you to help your friends and to improve and save
them; ask for the strength to do God's will, ask for his kingdom
of peace, love and eternal life to be established on earth. As
prayers of this kind are extremely rare, the invisible world will
say, 'Here's a being who is not like all the others; let's look after
his request first; let's give him what he's asking for!' Whereas
all the other things people ask for meet with the response: 'Be
patient, we'll study the question later.'

Of course, it does sometimes happen that your prayers are
answered very rapidly, but to your own detriment. Suppose that
your prayer for a very pretty wife is answered: you will never
know peace of mind again, because your lovely wife will be like
a garden full of ravishingly beautiful flowers, and a great many
other people will be attracted by their perfume and want to come
and enjoy it. And if, in addition, your wife is superficial and
frivolous, and you yourself are weak, jealous and suspicious, just
imagine what complications are in store for you! Your charming
wife will want to satisfy her vanity by showing off her beauty;
she will bring disaster on you, you will find yourself on the brink
of hell. What a price to pay for the small amount of joy she gives
you! Oh, believe me: I have nothing against pretty women! They

are an ornament to life and, therefore, very necessary; beauty is an attribute of God himself,[1] and beautiful women have inspired painters, sculptors, poets and musicians. But the sad thing is that most people pounce on beauty to devour it, instead of contemplating it from afar, and the result is that, in no time at all, there is no beauty left.

If you want your prayer to be answered promptly, you must ask for your freedom and that of others. When someone knocks insistently and importunately for purely material advantages, the invisible world knows that he is no better than a spoilt child who does not realize the consequences of what he is asking for and, knowing that he will certainly cry and regret it later on, they try to delay answering his request. But if you want to be sure of receiving a prompt answer to your prayer, ask for your own freedom and that of others.

I want to talk to you, now, about the eyes, ears and mouth from a different point of view.

Let's start with the eyes. You know that the eye is an almost spherical organ, with a slight convex bulge in the front. It consists of three membranes: the sclera, the front part of which forms the cornea; the choroid, the front of which forms the iris, and the retina, at the back of which is the macula lutea, the yellow spot which is the region of most acute vision. These three membranes represent the three worlds: physical, astral and mental (See Figure 35).

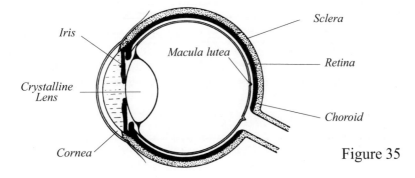

Figure 35

What interests us particularly, at the moment, are the light-sensitive cells of the retina, the rods and cones (See Figure 36).

The rods are sensitive only to the intensity of light, whereas the cones are sensitive to colour. It has been discovered that the retina of night-birds contains no cones, only rods. Owls like to hide their nests in a hole or behind the rafters of ruins or abandoned houses. Owls are ruled by Saturn; in fact the worst characteristics of this planet are manifested by owls which cannot bear the glow-worms that shine among the tall grasses on summer nights: they pursue them relentlessly.

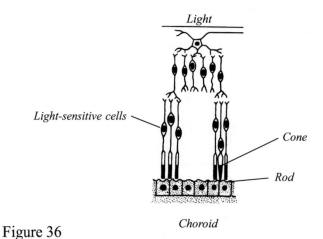

Figure 36

Christ said, *'Why do you look at the speck* in your brother's eye, but do not consider the plank in your own eye?'* and this means, 'Why do you look at other people's little weaknesses and never see your own, very obvious faults?' He who lives in the dark has only rods (that is to say, planks) in his eyes, so he cannot

---

* The Master was lecturing in French, and where English translations of the Bible use the words 'mote' or 'speck' in this context, French versions speak of a 'straw'. This must be remembered in order to understand the Master's later reference to straw and planks or beams.

see colours. But if we look at nature without seeing its colours we shall never understand either its beauty or its meaning.

The rods represent those who live in darkness, who are always criticizing and trying to destroy others; whereas the cones represent those who live in light and love, in harmony with the divine laws.

You know how men used to build their huts – and many still do, today – with a few planks or beams placed horizontally and vertically and with the spaces filled in with straw. Straw is what is left after the harvest; the part that is discarded. Wheat, therefore, represents the virtues, whereas straw represents the minor faults and failings that must be discarded. And the beams represent the capital sins.

A diagrammatic representation of a house consists of a triangle (the roof) and a square (the body of the house).

 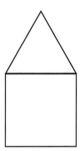

Figure 37

The triangle and the square symbolize spirit and matter, heaven and earth, for 3 is the number of the divine principles and 4 is the number of the four states of matter. The roof is above and the four walls below; a house also represents man himself, the 3 joined to the 4, which makes 7.[2]

A vertical section of a cone produces a triangle; the cross-section of a beam produces a square. The square and the triangle symbolize the two schools of thought which are in perpetual conflict in the world: the school of the spirit and that of matter, the school of love, wisdom and truth, and that of selfishness, callousness and violence. Those who try to impose their will on others for selfish, personal reasons are followers of the school of violence, the school of the beam. Those who, on the contrary, want to bring light, warmth and healing to others, who want to free their souls and lead them to the fountainhead of life, follow the teaching of the cone. These two schools – that of the rods and that of the cones – have existed ever since the world began; they are inherent in nature. Unfortunately, human beings never really try to understand the lessons that nature puts before them every day, everywhere, in even the smallest things.

Jesus knew perfectly well that he was surrounded by followers of the school of rods or beams. They were the Pharisees, Sadducees and scribes who wanted to kill him by means of earthly forces. When they decided to crucify him, they said: 'Since you claim to be the Son of God, we'll see what you make of the beams we're going to put you on', and they crucified him on two beams put together in the form of a cross. But Christ replied: 'You are learned men; you know the Cabbalah and you are applying the law of the number 4 which is the number of justice. If you are truly just, well and good, but if the law declares you unjust, then you must know what is in store for you.' The efficacy of a symbol applies in the three worlds, and he who behaves unjustly in the world of thought will have to suffer pain in the world of feeling and imprisonment in the physical world. Let's look at the number 4 in the three worlds:

♃ in the mental world;
+ in the astral world (the two opposing currents);
□ symbol of limitation on the physical plane.

4 is the number of Jupiter (♃), and Jupiter dwells in the sephirah *Chesed* in which the Archangel Tsadkiel (from *tsedek,*

justice and *El*, God) rules over the *Hashmalim*.[3] This is why people who are born under the influence of Jupiter often become judges.

The Pharisees did not understand Jesus' words, but later, after he had been crucified, everything that he had foretold came about: when the Roman Emperor Titus destroyed Jerusalem, he had all the leaders of the Jews crucified. Christ had told them: 'You use the methods of violence, the methods of the beams, and you will have to suffer the consequences', and everything happened just as he had said it would.

And now let's look at the cones. I have already told you that the frequencies of the vibrations of light form a continuum ranging from red, on the lowest end of the scale (and, lower still, infrared) to the higher frequencies of violet (and beyond that, of ultraviolet), and that this continuum can be represented as a cone (See Figure 19, chapter 3).

When I said that you must climb a spiritual mountain, I explained that the geometrical projection of a cone was a circle with a dot in the centre ⊙. The cone represents a spiral of light. The small cones in our eyes represent our potential spiritual capacity (contained in the symbolic cone) to see the realities of the world above.

All men wear glasses inwardly: some wear red glasses, others orange, yellow or green glasses, etc. What does this mean?

Those who wear red glasses are fond of eating and drinking and other sensual pleasures and, once they have eaten and drunk to their satisfaction, they are ready to go to war.

Those who wear orange glasses have a tendency to be individualistic and to keep to themselves; they think that men should live and act alone and show their independence.

Those who wear yellow glasses are fond of study; they reflect and reason and try to find solutions to their problems by intellectual means.

Those who wear green glasses have a tendency to believe that every problem in life can be dealt with by economic and financial means; they become businessmen.

Those who wear blue glasses believe that men need a philosophy based on religion; they work for peace among men and they are lovers of music, because music fosters peace.

Those who wear indigo glasses think that they have been specially chosen by providence to rule the world; they are priests and kings. Indigo is the colour of royalty and of the priesthood.

Those who wear violet glasses are the mystics who spend their lives adoring God in prayer, meditation and fasting.

The seven colours can be mixed and intermingled to give an infinite variety of shades. For instance, there are 40,000 shades of red alone!

Each colour is related to a particular point of view or domain in life,[4] but it is important to be capable of seeing all the different aspects of nature and of life. When we can do this, we are in the development of the cone; we are an eye which sees things clearly; the lenses in our spectacles are colourless, pure and transparent. Ideally, we should resemble the cones in our eyes and be capable of seeing all the colours at the same time, instead of being like the rods which can distinguish only different shades of grey. You all know that, in the course of history, many millions of human beings have been the victims of men who had a very narrow point of view, men, in other words, who could distinguish only one colour. How many errors have been committed – as often by religious and spiritual people as by materialists – simply because of a lack of breadth of vision!

Man must free himself from the narrowness of his mental constructs and rise above all divergencies of opinion; in other words, he must look at things through colourless glasses. Christ said, *'Blessed are the pure in heart, for they shall see God.'*[5] What connection is there between the heart and the eye? The same phenomenon operates in the heart as in the crystalline lens: both have to be accommodated. If the lens is flattened one cannot see properly, and if the heart is 'flattened' one cannot see properly either. Someone who does not look with the eyes of love cannot see all the magnificent qualities of others or the beauties of nature and, not only is he unable to see other peoples qualities, but he is always criticizing and trying to put to rights the Creator of all things. How often one hears people complaining that nature and life have been very badly designed and that if they had been in the Lord's place they would have dome a much better job! Let me tell you at once that, if that is your attitude, you will never enter into the kingdom of the mysteries for, in spite of what most people think, the designs of nature are inexpressibly intelligent and apt.

You must try to look at only the good qualities of other people. Tell me, what advantage have you ever gained from looking at their defects? You must realize that if you always think about other people's faults, not only will you make them worse, but the attention you give them will be like a magnet by which you draw them to yourself. Very few are aware of the havoc created by this habit of dwelling on the negative aspects of people and things. In fact, many very 'civilized' people think that it is a sign of superiority to be critical. So many friendships have been destroyed, so many bonds have been broken because of this tendency to look at other people's faults, to dwell on their vices and weaknesses, even to take pleasure in studying their lives in order to ferret them out. A wise man endeavours to see both sides of people, the good as well as the bad; in this way he avoids certain inconveniences and, at the same time, helps others to subdue their negative aspects and to strengthen and enrich their positive aspects, their higher nature. This does not mean that a wise man is blind, or that he is taken in by appearances; it simply means that he considers that the essence of a person or a thing is the good that is in them and, by concentrating on it, he can draw strength from it and reinforce it both in himself and in them. This is why all beings are attracted to someone like this: they sense that the seeds of their divine nature are free to grow and flourish in his presence.

You may get pleasure out of dwelling on other people's faults, but it is a pleasure that will have veryserious consequences. He who gives way to this tendency is a danger to all those around him and, above all, to himself; he is always discontented, he amplifies the least little imperfection, he is in revolt against himself and everyone else. And if he is asked to give his opinion about what should be done to improve a situation, you will find that the solutions he proposes are worse than those he has criticized so freely. In Bulgaria there is a story about the gypsies who suffered so much from the cold in winter that they asked God to do away with it altogether. God did as they asked, and to begin with they were very pleased with the result. But then, as there was no more cold weather in winter to kill the insects, they proliferated to such an extent and did so much damage, that the gypsies begged God to bring back the winter. La Fontaine also has a fable about a peasant who thought that nature had organized things very badly in making tiny little acorns grow on the huge limbs of an oak tree, whereas pumpkins hang on the fragile stem of a vine. Then, one day, he was hit on the head by an acorn falling from an oak, and he realized what would have happened to him if a pumpkin had fallen on him from such a height! He was forced to admit that nature was, after all, wiser than he was.

We have to climb to the summit of the spiritual mountain, symbolized by the cone, so as to learn to see things from above. Imagine, for instance, that you are an eminent professor, and you have a little boy who has climbed up to the top of a tree, in the garden. Suddenly, he calls out, 'Dad, Dad, I can see two people coming up the road.' You ask him, 'Can you see who they are?' 'Yes, it's Aunt and Uncle, and they've got some presents for us!' The child is smaller than you, he is not as learned as you, but he can see what you cannot see from where you are standing. What does this mean? It means that some philosophers look at life from such an inadequate point of view that they can neither see nor understand things correctly. On the other hand, there are

people who have very little education but who have a point of
view which enables them to see things that are hidden to the eyes
of the learned. We read these words in the Gospel: *'I thank you,
Father, Lord of heaven and earth, because you have hidden these
things from the wise and the intelligent and have revealed them
to infants.'* Why? Because children love to climb up to the top of
rocks and trees. And then, too, one sometimes meets people who
are not at all learned but who understand truth, who feel it. As
for me, I am like a child of twelve, my intellectual faculties are
far less impressive than yours but I have been placed on a peak
from which I can see a great many things.

Our point of view is often more important than our gifts or
talents. If we look at things from a very inferior point of view,
however intelligent and knowledgeable we may be, we shall
never see them as they are, so we shall never understand them
properly. On the other hand, somebody who is totally uneducated
can have a point of view which enables him to see the miracles
of nature. Examine yourself and find out what your point of view
is. A good point of view is worth more than all your personal
capacities.[6]

And, as we are on the subject, I would like to say something
about the dangerous habit many people have of looking at things
that are declining: the setting sun, falling leaves, etc. Many people
are lost in admiration at the marvellous colours of a sunset, but
think that it is stupid to go and contemplate the sunrise every
morning. And in the autumn, when the leaves begin to fall from
the trees, they find the spectacle magnificent and melancholy,
but in the spring, when the whole of nature is bursting into new
life, how many go out of doors to admire it and watch the buds
opening? Not many! This is what I mean when I say that people
look for God at night. Yes, for nature has its own days and nights;
until noon it is daytime; after noon it is already the beginning of
night. Go and contemplate nature during the day; that is when
she is disposed to give. If you want to steep yourself in a pure,
vivifying atmosphere and imbibe the treasures it contains, you

must go out in the morning, as early as possible. This is why, in our teaching, we go to watch the sunrise during the spring.[7]

And now, let me say something about the ears.

The ears represent wisdom and, in contrast to the eyes and the mouth, which are alternately active and passive, the ears are wholly passive. You all know about the activity of the mouth (especially of the tongue!); the eyes, too, can sometimes be very active; they can seduce or slay someone with a look. But the ears are never active, except when you pay attention and, even then, their activity is a passive one, for all they do is receive sounds.

I have seen people who went to see the Master and who, instead of listening and learning from him, spent their time showing off their knowledge and quoting from all the books they had read. Although he was sometimes unable to get in a word of his own, the Master always listened to them with extraordinary patience, smiling gently all the while! In the end, these people finally realized that they were doing all the talking and that if they did not keep quiet and wait for the Master to speak, they would not learn anything. And what was their surprise when they found that they learned more from him in a few minutes than from several years of studying books, simply because they had adopted a receptive attitude which enabled them to receive the Master's emanations.[8]

A disciple must learn to put himself in the state that we call 'passive' and which you must, on no account, take to be laziness or inertia. On the contrary, although it seems to be an absence of activity, this state of passivity is an intense form of activity. It requires tremendous self-discipline and considerable knowledge of psychology to reach this state... more than most people are capable of. But those who do manage to do so are able to hear, through all the uproar and commotion of life, the voice of their soul, which is none other than the voice of God.

This state of passivity can be either beneficial or harmful, depending on circumstances and the influences at work in one's environment. It is a state in which we receive, imbibe and absorb all the influences around us, whether good or evil; whereas when we are in a state of activity, by contrast, it is we who project and radiate forces onto our environment. Depending on the circumstances, therefore, we must learn to be either active and emissive or passive and receptive.[9] If you are in the presence of actively evil influences, you must protect yourself and prevent them from affecting you by being positive and emissive. But if the influences surrounding you are beneficial and propitious, you must be receptive, otherwise you will get no benefit from them. When you are in the presence of corrupt, evil people you must be active, positive and emissive, but when you are in the presence of a being of great purity, nobility and kindness, an initiate, you must be receptive. Unfortunately, you often do just the opposite, and then you are surprised and distressed to find that so many good conditions seem to be destroyed and there is no respite from your torment.

The organ of Corti teaches us that, if we want to hear and understand others, we must learn to respond to their vibrations, to all the thoughts and feelings that emanate from them; we must learn to resonate in harmony with them. If we are incapable of resonating in harmony with the great masters we shall never understand them. But we can vibrate in harmony with them if we learn to leave the short strings of our soul free to respond to the subtlest vibrations of the universe. He who knows how to listen like this lives on a deeper level and comes so close to the subtlest beings in creation that he begins to be capable of tuning in to their vibrations.

Wisdom lies in being capable of listening to the still, small voice that speaks within us. We have no difficulty in hearing the thunderous voice of a hungry stomach calling for food or that of our sexual organs clamouring for satisfaction, but when a small voice says, 'Don't do that...', we tell it to keep quiet. Yes, and then it is time for the 'third teacher' to enter the picture!

The first teacher, the Sun, teaches by means of our eyes; he attempts to reach our intelligence by showing us truth. But we say: 'Who knows if that is really the truth? It may be nothing more than an illusion', and we go on living as we have always lived. The second teacher is Venus, love, and she tries to touch our hearts, but we refuse to understand her any better than the first. As for the third teacher, Saturn, we are all familiar with him; he comes with a big stick (a beam!), with the intention of beating a little sense into us! All the blows that life deals us represent this third teacher. Those who understand and hear the voice of wisdom at once have no need to suffer any longer, but those who cannot hear, still need to have their ears pulled. And since we mention it, why do you think we talk about pulling a person's ears if he is not wise? Where do you suppose the expression comes from? If you want to avoid all the grief and distress that the third teacher always brings with him, there is no other way than to pull your own ears, every day, and persuade yourself to listen! In this way, little by little, you will become wiser. Does this seem childish? You may be sure that it is not!

The third teacher is about to visit the world,* and all men will see how severe and implacable he is: he causes terrible upheavals, he tramples the proud underfoot, he topples gigantic constructions that everyone thought were unshakeable, he overthrows men's most firmly entrenched beliefs and opinions. Epidemics and wars, famines and disease all represent this third teacher. But you must not think that he is ill-intentioned; the truth is that he is motivated by the noblest intentions: to bring God's rebellious children back to a right understanding, to restore them to their heavenly Father and the knowledge of his wisdom and love. The warnings of initiates and all the good advice of the wise

---

* This lecture was given in 1938; the Master Omraam Mikhaël Aïvanhov was referring to the Second World War which was imminent (Editor's note).

are often without effect, but when this third instructor comes on the scene with his stick, unruly children begin to take notice and understand!

The invisible world has already sent many great masters and initiates to instruct mankind, but men say, 'I'm sorry but I'm busy. I don't have time to listen to you. I have a wife and children and some urgent business to attend to...' It is a repetition of the parable of the rich man who sent his servants to invite all his friends to a great banquet. But each in turn had an excuse for not accepting his invitation: 'I have bought five yoke of oxen, and I am going to test them. I ask you to have me excused.' Or, 'I have found a very pretty wife, and I'm going to be married today...' They were all very busy with things that seemed important but which were, in reality, useless or, at best, of only minor importance. And you, too, are often busy with futile occupations which prevent you from listening to what an initiate teaches you.

Listen now to a few pages from the history of Bulgaria. During the course of the centuries, heaven has sent many initiates to Bulgaria. Nine centuries ago it was the turn of the Bogomils, but nobody would listen to them; they were persecuted and massacred and driven from the country. But Bulgaria was very severely punished, because these initiates represented the lamps of our country and the people tried to extinguish them. Thieves don't break into a house when all the lights are on for fear of being seen; they wait until the lights are out and the occupants of the house safely asleep, before sneaking in. And the same is true for a country or an individual: if you turn out your lights (the virtues), you will be broken into by thieves who will bind you hand and foot; in other words, you will lose your freedom and all that is most precious to you. The thieves are illness, distress, negative thoughts, sorrows of all kinds. Only light can protect us, it is the only true safeguard: for where there is light, no one can come near you without being seen. So, when the Bulgarians drove out the Bogomils and put out their light, the country was attacked by thieves and, for five hundred years, the people lived under the domination of the Turks. Thousands and thousands of men were hanged or had their heads cut off before, at long last, the invisible world gave the country its freedom again. In every country, at some period of its history, there have been beings who taught a doctrine of love and light to which men have refused to listen, with the result that disasters rained down on them. This is something that you must realize: whenever we put out a light, whether it be in ourselves, in our own bodies or in our country, thieves will inevitably take advantage of the dark to break in.

Before I started this talk, somebody asked me, 'How can we develop the gift of clairvoyance?'

True clairvoyance is the ability to see God in the whole of nature,[10] to see wisdom and reason and all the higher realities. Some people, even scientists, complain that they have looked everywhere for God and never been able to find him. Obviously, if they expected to meet him as one meets another human being, they were in no danger of finding him! God is truth, wisdom, love and beauty and he can be seen if our eyes are not closed, if they are not full of beams. If we look for him in the dark, there will always be a beam in our eyes; we need to have cones, not only in our eyes but also in our souls.

There used to be a clairvoyant in Bulgaria who knew the Master. She was called Cortez, and she had a truly remarkable gift that enabled her to see both the past and the future. Wherever she went, she was always surrounded by a crowd of people and, sometimes, she would stop a passer-by in the street and start to reprimand him. At the time, I was too young to understand all this, but my mother witnessed any number of scenes similar to the one I want to tell you about. One day, Cortez stopped a man who was out for a walk with his two children. 'Wait', she said; 'those are your children, aren't they?' 'Yes, they're my children', replied the man, a little put out. 'And they're dumb?' asked Cortez. 'Yes.' 'But do you know why they're dumb?' she insisted. 'No', said the man; 'I don't know.' 'Well I do!' replied

Cortez; 'Before your children were born you committed some crimes and stole things. One day, you stole some sheep and, in order to get them away, you had to go past a place where they would have been heard if they had bleated, so you cut out their tongues. That is why your children were born dumb. And now you must make reparation and beg heaven to forgive you.' Then Cortez explained to the man that he must buy some cows and give them to the person he had robbed and that, if he did not do so, he would be punished even more severely. The man followed her advice and his children recovered the power of speech!

It is possible to develop powers of clairvoyance, but we must not try to do so before acquiring purity. Christ said, *'Blessed are the pure in heart, for they shall see God.'* He who is not pure cannot be clairvoyant: he will only see the monsters that surround him and other people; he will see that men are often false friends, that their hearts are full of treachery and deceit, and he will have foreknowledge of every disaster before it happens. In other words, he will be able to see things on the level that he himself has reached, but very little else. This is why the best way to develop one's clairvoyance is to cultivate spiritual love and purity in oneself.[11]

I know, of course, that people teach all kinds of other methods: they tell you to gaze into crystal balls or magic mirrors, to use certain plants that are common in Mexico or elsewhere, to get someone to hypnotize you, etc., etc. But all these methods are bad and some are dangerous, and I do not advise you to use them. Why do people always want powers of magic and divination when they are still weak, jealous and avaricious, full of anger, passion and cupidity? The entities of the invisible world are not at all pleased to be observed or disturbed by unworthy intruders. Some of them love human beings and welcome them warmly, but others are hostile and ready to pursue anyone who tries to force an entry into their regions for his own dubious reasons. Intruders always incur the animosity of the beings of the invisible world.

Many occultists come to a sorry end because of their ambition to become rich or make a name for themselves as clairvoyants, initiates or magicians. They don't know how to defend themselves against the attacks of beings who resent their intrusion into their domain. To begin with, these attacks take the form of unnatural or perverse desires, but they often degenerate and can even turn to madness. The beings of the invisible world have already eliminated a great many human victims. There is altogether too much occult literature available in the world today, and this is very grave, for it provides nourishment for entities of the lowest planes, and gives human beings the arms they need in order to subjugate their fellow men. This literature divulges the means and methods to use in order to enter hitherto unknown regions and make contact with their inhabitants and, in doing so, has brought on its adepts every kind of misfortune. The annals of Esoteric Science tell us that several races of man have been destroyed because they practised demonism and black magic, and the depravity of men is leading the world in the same direction today. The fate of Atlantis will be repeated in our day, but in another form. In the past it was water that destroyed the continent of Atlantis, but next time it will be fire in all its forms, that will be the executioner.

Instead of teaching men the methods of the past, we must lead them towards a new understanding and new methods. Don't evoke the old images, don't disturb the ancient dust of the underworld, otherwise you will awaken sleeping powers which will repeat the disasters of the past. You will not give mankind a new culture by archeological excavations in ancient tombs, nor by publishing any number of volumes about the prodigious science of the past, nor by disturbing spiders and scorpions in underground crypts. The ignorance of those who do this kind of research causes them to trigger terrifyingly powerful fluidic forces, without their being in the least aware of it. And, once liberated, these forces spread, insinuate themselves into unresisting minds and spirits and lead men to revive the past and repeat the same faults all over again. I am not opposed to scientific research, but archeological research has nothing very useful to teach us. There are other ways of getting to know the spirit of extinct civilizations without having to study the scattered fragments that they have left behind. Those who are ignorant of other methods are obliged to resort to these imperfect means but, instead of informing them correctly, these means only mislead them further. There is an underground world in which all knowledge from time immemorial is stored: here can be found the archives of mankind; a true disciple has no need to go and search through archeological remains to find out about man's past.

A true master will tell you: 'Put aside all these dusty, mouldy things that are already dead and buried! Concentrate on what is luminous and alive!' Each day, the sun is new, the whole of nature is new. The very fact that something is already in a state of decay is proof enough that it does not contain the truth. That which is true cannot be destroyed; time cannot touch it. The passage of hundreds and thousands of years cannot affect that which is eternal, and it is that that we are looking for. That which is true is here, before our eyes, all round us, in us. If we understand the new currents that are manifesting themselves in the world and bringing us new life, every day, we shall abandon many illusions based on so-called scientific knowledge.

But, to get back to the question of clairvoyance, I repeat: it is better to begin by working at yourself, at your own purity, first of all; once you yourself are transformed, complete clairvoyance will be given to you, almost in spite of yourself. When God gives something, he gives it in abundance.

There is a story that a Master once had a disciple who was eager to learn the first lesson of initiation. The Master said to him, 'Go to the cemetery and insult the dead; tell them how stupid and wicked they are, and then come back and tell me how they reacted.' The disciple went off to the cemetery and started shouting insults at the dead, but the dead said never a word. When he went back to his Master and told him this, the Master said, 'Perhaps you didn't go about it properly. Perhaps they didn't hear you. Go back again, but this time, do just the opposite: praise and flatter them.' So the disciple returned to the cemetery but, once again, the dead responded by silence, even to the most extravagant compliments. The disciple went back to his Master and said, 'They still didn't answer me.' 'Excellent', said his Master; 'Now you know the first lesson of Initiation: when someone insults you, keep silent, and when someone flatters you, keep silent. Be like the dead: deaf and dumb.' This is a very important lesson.

Last Saturday, when I was talking to you about the mouth, I told you that the leaves of trees also possessed tiny mouths called stomata which are their medium of exchange with the environment. Through the action of light on the chlorophyll, xanthophyll and carotene contained in the leaves, the raw mineral solution absorbed by the roots of the plant is converted into sap. And this is what happens in our mouths: our mouths contain glands which secrete substances similar to chlorophyll, xanthophyll and carotene and, when we eat in light and warmth, that is to say, when the light of our thoughts and the warmth of our love acts on our food, it undergoes a spiritual transformation; but when we chew it without thinking what we are doing and without love for the Creator who gave it to us, no transformation is effected and what we absorb is simply raw material that has received some chemical preparation. If you eat like everyone else, in the midst of noise, disorder and agitation, the nutritional processes involved will be purely physical and chemical. Whereas, when you eat in silence, in a spirit of love and gratitude, you raise the process to the level of alchemy and sublimation.[12]

And the same is true of all our activities, even our professional work or studies. If we are not attentive to our work or if we don't love what we are studying, for instance, it will not be of much benefit to us. Let's suppose that you have to work closely with someone who always rubs you up the wrong way. We might say – symbolically speaking – that our mouth refuses to absorb him, that he is a spiritually indigestible raw material! But if we possess the warmth and strength of love and light, our spiritual glands will start to function and then we shall find that we can 'swallow' him; he will no longer 'stick in our throat' or give us psychic indigestion! Whereas if we keep trying to digest him without the help of light and warmth, we shall only weaken and exhaust ourselves. With warmth and light we can transform whatever comes to us in a raw state, whether it be food, other human beings, influences or objects. Until such time as we are full of light and warmth, our spiritual mouth will find these raw materials very unpalatable but, with the help of warmth and light, we shall be able to transform them.

When you look at nature, you see that plants feed on minerals, animals eat plants and human beings eat animals. And this might lead you to wonder who eats human beings. The answer is: the angels. Yes, perhaps you have never thought of that: men are food for the angels. Obviously, we are not actually eaten by the angels, but they feed on our fruits, on the thoughts and feelings we produce, exactly as we feed on animal products: milk, honey, eggs, butter, etc. But if the food we produce is not good they will not accept it; in fact, if it is bad, other angels, the angels of evil, will come and feed on us.

When Christ announced the terrible events that were to befall the world, one of his disciples asked him where they would take place, and he replied: *'Wherever the corpse is, there the vultures will gather.'* This is the law that I have been talking about. If you have corpses within you (putrid, rotten feelings or thoughts), food for the vultures, that is to say, the lower beings of the invisible world.[13] You will, perhaps, ask, 'But how do these creatures scent the whereabouts of these thoughts and feelings?' Well, when you have some honey in your room, how do the ants find out that it is there and come and eat it? Ants have special antennae (in fact, it was they that first invented the wireless)! Like bees, ants come from the planet Venus; they are an exception in nature. But if your house is swarming with ants, it is nothing to worry about because, tiny though they are, snakes are terrified of them: if we are inhabited by ants, therefore, snakes will flee from them. I shall be very glad if you are capable of interpreting this symbol.

Bees are very fond of flowers. A bee symbolizes the faithful disciple who prepares nectar in his soul for the angels to gather and transform into honey. It is said that the prayers of the saints rise before God as a sweet perfume. This perfume is God's nourishment. For the moment, you cannot really understand this but, one day, the subtle interconnections between all the different aspects of the universe will be clearer to you.

And now, I want to say a little more about the eyes, the ears and the mouth. We receive light through our eyes and sound through our ears. What an extraordinary relationship there is between the eyes and the ears! Take the way in which light and sound are propagated: light travels freely through a vacuum, less easily through air, even less easily through water, in which it is refracted and from which it is partly reflected, and less easily still through solids. With sound, however, it is just the opposite: it cannot travel through empty space, it needs a material medium; sound is more easily transmitted through liquids than through air and more easily still through solids than through liquids. In respect to the medium of transmission, therefore, light is the exact opposite of sound. It descends from the regions of greatest subtlety, making its way ever more laboriously through regions of greater and greater density until it reaches solid matter. Sound, on the contrary, originates on the level of solid matter and rises to the subtler regions, gradually decreasing in intensity until it fades away altogether in emptiness.

The power of sound (the word) lies in the realm of matter, but light, which is powerful in the realm of the spirit, existed before sound. This is why our ears and eyes are designed in accordance with different laws, the one being related to wisdom and the other to truth. Light illuminates the forms and colours which reveal beauty, and beauty is an expression of the truth that formed the eyes. Sound (the word) is related to the ears, the ears to wisdom and wisdom to the mouth, for it is the mouth that utters words. The mouth, ears and eyes form a triangle, and many different combinations of the three are possible. The eyes contemplate, the ears hear and the mouth tells what the eyes have seen and the ears heard. And herein lies the secret of the intimate relationship between love, wisdom and truth.

And now I want to give you the following exercise: as soon as you wake up in the morning, you should open your eyes consciously, turn your gaze inwards to your inner eye and listen to the voice that is speaking within you. If you do this you will hear your programme for this new day. But the three angles of the triangle must be included in this exercise; in other words, let your mouth act in conjunction with your eyes and ears by saying the following formula: 'Thank You, Lord, for giving me good health today. May my day be blessed. Help me to do your will.'

Ordinarily, the first words most people pronounce on getting up in the morning are words of complaint. Husbands are exasperated with their wives because their shirts have not come back from the laundry or they cannot find their cuff-links or their socks, or they complain that the coffee is cold, etc. In other words, as soon as they get up they start complaining! This is a very bad habit.

There was once a king who had two daughters. The eldest was very ugly but she had the gift of words; she could express absolutely magnificent thoughts in the most delightful way. The second was exceptionally pretty but she had a wicked tongue and was always hurting people's feelings. The situation was very awkward for their father who always felt rather ashamed of his daughters in front of visitors, especially if they were the kings of neighbouring kingdoms. Besides, he worried about how he was ever going to marry them off. One day, he consulted a wise man about the problem. 'Your Majesty', said the sage; 'Send a messenger into the town tomorrow and tell him to bring before you the first two men he meets. You shall marry your daughters to them.' The next day, the king followed the wise man's advice and sent a messenger into the town. When he brought the first two men he had met into the royal presence, the king was intrigued to find that one of them was blind and the other deaf. When he told the sage this, he exclaimed, 'But that's perfect! Marry the blind man to your ugly daughter and the deaf man to the pretty one.' Once again, the king did as the wise man advised and the blind man, bewitched by the beautiful things his wife said, was only sorry that he could not see her, for he imagined that she was as lovely as her words. As for the deaf man, he was lost in admiration of his wife's beautiful face, and regretted only that he could not hear what she said, for it must certainly be as sweet as her face. But what would have happened if the blind man could have seen and the deaf man heard?

It is fortunate for us that we are sometimes a little shortsighted or hard of hearing when we are confronted with unpleasantness. As a matter of fact, men are not over-fond of the truth. A husband will say to his wife, 'Tell me you love me. I know it's not true, but say it anyway; it does me good to hear it!' Or he will say, 'I know that you're not specially pretty, but if you would only put some make-up on, I'd enjoy looking at you!' No, men do not love truth! And yet, every time we see our own eyes in the mirror, we should take the opportunity to give thanks and ally ourselves with truth. And when we listen with our ears, we should ally ourselves with wisdom. And, when we taste something in our mouth, we should ally ourselves with love. In this way we can become a living triangle. A wise man can look at this triangle and know exactly what we are. Depending on the form of our mouth, ears and eyes, and on their size and position in relation to the normal position, a sage can tell exactly where we stand in relation to love, wisdom and truth.

You know that we all have two eyes, two ears and a mouth. Yes, but, in reality, we have three eyes, three ears and three mouths. The third eye, the mystical eye, is situated in the centre of the forehead; the third ear is situated in the throat, and the second mouth is situated at the top of the skull: it is the chakra of a thousand petals.[14] This is the higher mouth with which we speak and eat on the spiritual level; it is the centre that absorbs, prays and receives nourishment in the divine world. I shall not talk to you about the third mouth today.

The planet earth also has organs similar to ours. Its higher mouth is represented by the highest mountains. The earth is in contact with heaven by means of its highest peaks.

Let us ally ourselves with love, wisdom and truth.
By means of our mouth we shall taste divine love,
By means of our ears we shall listen to divine wisdom,
By means of our eyes we shall see divine truth.

Paris, 5 March 1938

Notes
1. See *'Know Thyself' – Jnana Yoga,* Complete Works, vol. 18, chap. 1: 'Beauty'.
2. See *The Philosopher's Stone – in the Gospels and in Alchemy,* Izvor Coll. n° 241, chap. 9: 'The Work of the Alchemist: 3 over 4'.
3. See *Angels and other Mysteries of The Tree of Life,* Izvor Coll. n° 236, chap. 3: 'The Angelic Hierarchies'.
4. See *The Splendour of Tiphareth – The Yoga of the Sun,* Complete Works, vol. 10, chap. 11: 'The Spirits of the Seven Lights'.
5. See *The Mysteries of Yesod – Foundations of the Spiritual Life,* Complete Works, vol 7, Part II, chap. 10: 'Blessed are the Pure in Heart'.
6. See *'In Spirit and in Truth',* Izvor Coll. n° 235, chap. 1: 'The Framework of the Universe'.
7. See *The Splendour of Tiphareth – The Yoga of the Sun,* Complete Works, vol. 10.
8. See *What is a Spiritual Master?,* Izvor Coll. n° 207, chap. 8: 'The Disciple and His Master'.

9. See *Love and Sexuality,* Complete Works, vol. 15, chap. 17: 'Emptiness and Fullness: the Holy Grail', and *Looking into the Invisible,* Izvor Coll. n° 228, chap. 3: 'The Entrance to the Invisible World: From Yesod to Tiphareth', and chap. 4: 'Clairvoyance: Activity and Receptivity'.

10. See *The Faith That Moves Mountains,* Izvor Coll. n° 238, chap. 12: 'God in Creation'.

11. See *Looking into the Invisible,* Izvor Coll. n° 228, chap. 6: 'Love and Your Eyes Will be Opened', and chap. 9: 'The Higher Degrees of Clairvoyance'.

12. See *The Path of Silence,* Izvor Coll. n° 229, chap. 4: 'Make Your Meals an Exercise in Silence'.

13. See *Life Force,* Complete Works, vol. 5, chap. 7: 'Unwanted Guests'.

14. See *Man's Subtle Bodies and Centres,* Izvor Coll. n° 219, chap. 6: 'The Chakras'.

Chapter Seven

PETER DEUNOV, THE MASTER OF THE
UNIVERSAL WHITE BROTHERHOOD IN BULGARIA

The Master Peter Deunov (1938)

This evening I want to talk to you about my Master, Peter Deunov. I could never say all that there is to say about him in one lecture, but I shall try to be as clear and simple as possible and to describe facts and actual experiences, which should give you a very good idea of what he is like.

The Master Peter Deunov is a being of very exalted spirituality whose whole life has been an example of purity, wisdom and intelligence. For many years, now, he has lived and taught at a place near Sofia called *Izgrev* (which means sunrise), and many of his disciples live there, too, in sunny little houses which are surrounded by gardens without fences. It is as though all the houses were in one big park.

By word and example, and by the power radiating from him, the Master has accomplished wonders in those around him; several thousand men and women, both Bulgarians and foreigners, have become his disciples. His teaching, based on the harmonious laws of nature, offers numerous psychological and pedagogical methods capable of improving the lives of human beings, and seventy volumes of lectures, taken down in shorthand by his disciples, have already been published.

Music and singing have a very special place in the Master's teaching, for music is seen as an extremely potent means in allying oneself with the constructive forces of nature and recovering one's physical and psychic equilibrium. The Master himself has composed many songs and created a special form of rhythmic dance called paneurhythmy, which can be performed by hundreds of disciples dancing in a vast circle round an orchestra. The Paneurhythmy is danced out of doors, in the morning, after the sunrise. It has a very beneficial influence on the nervous system; each gesture, although extremely simple, has great plastic beauty and corresponds to a profound understanding of the psychic structure of human beings and the laws of acoustics.[1] The Master has also given us some gymnastic exercises to be done in the morning, preferably before the paneurhythmy. Each movement of these exercises is designed to improve our health and strengthen the body by harmonizing our cells.

The Master encourages his disciples to fast. Once a week, from Thursday after lunch until Friday noon, all the disciples fast, taking no solid food for twenty-four hours. During this time, as a further aid to purification, they drink only very hot, boiled water which is conducive to the elimination of wastes. Those who fast for five or ten days or more do so according to the Master's instructions and under his personal guidance.

The Master's teaching excludes the use of tobacco, alcohol and meat. By eating their vegetarian meals in common, the disciples develop an ever keener awareness of the power inherent in brotherly behaviour.

In the summer, the whole Brotherhood gathers round the Master at the summer camp in the Rila mountains. This site was specially chosen by him because, geologically, these are the oldest peaks on earth. From time immemorial, temples of the highest initiations existed on the Rila mountains, until events which it would take too long to explain, obliged the initiates to transport their temples to Tibet. For several weeks, the Brotherhood camps up there, near the seven lakes of Rila. To get up there, we have to undertake a long climb on foot. Imagine, if you will, that we are with the brothers and sisters, on our way up to the camp. After climbing for seven hours we come out of the forest and reach the shores of the first lake. Far above us we can see the sheer cliff on top of which is the camp. Up there, several brothers and sisters have already arrived and are preparing everything for the rest of us: hot water for drinks and baths, fires, meals and tents. From up above, they see our group and wave to greet us and welcome us with their song. The air echoes to the enthusiastic sounds of marching songs, and our hearts overflow with a tremendous sense of joy as we climb up the last slopes leading to the camp.

As the days go by, new groups of brothers and sisters join us. Many of them are young, but there are also a good number of old people who have no hesitation in coming to renew their youth up here and rejoice in the presence of their Master. At dawn, when everybody is still sound asleep in their tents, we suddenly hear the sound of a violin rousing us gently from sleep with the music of the song 'Wake up brother, and come and see the sunrise!' Then we get up, wash and make our way in silence up a narrow path which leads to the place we call 'the rock of prayer' from which we can see the sun rising. The air is very pure and the day is just dawning.

It is very moving to see the long column of brothers and sisters climbing up there in silence. Once at the top, we find ourselves on a natural rocky platform. Each one picks a place to sit and concentrate while waiting for the sun to rise. When the Master arrives we all stand to greet him and then sit down again and return to our meditation and prayers, endeavouring to draw into ourselves the etheric forces emanating from every corner of the horizon. The appearance of the sun is greeted with a song in its honour as we feel our souls swelling with immense joy. All of nature, all the rocks, trees, rivers and lakes vibrate in unison with the life force streaming from the sun, and our voices join in prayer as we raise our souls to the Lord. Prayer is more favourably received when it is spoken in the pure air of the mountain tops, and comes from a brain that is fully awake and a heart overflowing with joy. After the songs and prayers, the Master gives a talk in which he points out to the disciples the beauty of a life lived according to reason, the great wisdom concealed in the least details of nature and the ideal that each one must strive to attain: to work for the kingdom of heaven, to be a conductor of divine life.

After the Master's talk we go down to the camp, where we do the breathing exercises recommended by the Master and which are designed to develop both our physical and psychic capacities. After that, we do the gymnastics and dance the paneurhythmy on a broad plain by the shores of another lake. Several hundred disciples dance and sing in a huge circle, in the centre of which stands the orchestra with the Master. The Master is now seventy-four but none of his disciples can equal him in beauty, vigour or lightness of step. His gestures are supple and harmonious and his whole person radiates such power that none can remain insensible to it. His presence in the centre of the circle gives a tremendous impetus to all his disciples. After the paneurhythmy we stream back to the camp where we are free to have breakfast, work or go for a walk, as we please.

At noon we gather again in one big circle in the middle of the camp where the meal is distributed from the huge cauldrons and saucepans in which it has been cooked. Each day a small group of disciples takes it in turns to prepare and serve the midday meal. We eat in silence, in a spirit of joy and meditation. After the meal we are again free to do what we please. In the afternoon, the Master gives a talk or, sometimes, leads an excursion to other peaks in the Rila mountains. Sometimes, we walk for fourteen hours in a single day but, thanks to the Master who has shown us how to keep going for a long time without tiring, we are never really worn out.

In the evening, after supper, we light a big fire in the middle of the camp ground and sit round it, praying and singing the choral songs composed by the Master. Our great desire is for him to come down from his tent in the highest part of the camp, and join us round the blazing fire. Night falls, and we continue to

sing with great ardour, glancing up from time to time towards the
Master's tent in the hope of seeing the glimmer of light that will
tell us that our wish will be granted. All of a sudden the signal
is seen, our joy overflows and we strike up the song entitled
'Greetings to the Master': 'Oh Lord, You are my Master; let me
follow in your footsteps.' And now, the lantern, held aloft by a
brother, can be seen moving through the night, coming slowly
down the path leading to the camp fire. At last the Master is there,
the circle of brothers and sisters opens to give him a place by
the fire and closes behind him and the songs begin again... The
silence and immensity of the blue night sky, studded with stars,
seem to share in our intense mystical emotions. After the songs,
some of the brothers and sisters recite poetry or play the violin
or the guitar. But ten o'clock is approaching; the Master stands
and we all recite a prayer together, giving thanks for the blessings
received during the day, and, at last, it is time to separate and go
to our tents to sleep.

But there are always a few who stay by the fire and gaze at
the starry sky and the reflection of the moon on the still surface
of the lake.[2] A marvellous sense of peace comes over them as
they feel themselves to be in perfect union with the universe,
and their life takes on an extraordinary significance that they
will never forget. Later, when the others are already asleep in the
camp, they wend their way back to their tents to sleep until the
violin calls them again, at dawn, to live a new day in the light.

During these periods up in the mountains, the Master used
often to lead an excursion through rain and snow to the top of
Mount Musala; it was a way of putting our faith and endurance
to the test. The storm would be raging all round us; the rocks and
the ground under our feet would be so charged with electricity
that we could hardly bear the currents. Water flowed over us
and sparks flew from our hair and from the beards of some of
the brothers, but we continued without a murmur of complaint,
guided by the Master who always showed a most stoic endurance
and tremendous agility. How can I describe our feelings on these

occasions? Only those who have lived through these hours of physical and moral stress can understand how they temper the soul and spirit.

After a month or two of this kind of life we went back to our daily occupations in the towns, feeling ourselves to be transformed and better able to help those around us by word and example. We tried to show them that if only men would understand that good will, love and brotherhood were the very foundations of life, they would be capable of living differently, of creating the kingdom of God on earth.*

What is a master?[3] A master is someone who has achieved control, mastery of all his thoughts, feelings and acts. Perhaps you will say that that is nothing much, but you would be wrong: in point of fact, it is everything! To achieve complete control of all one's thoughts, feelings and acts implies the use of special methods, a special discipline and a profound knowledge not only of the structure of a human being, but also of the forces at work within him and the correspondences between his being (his organs and his several bodies) and the different realms of nature. To be master of oneself implies, also, that one is familiar with the entities of the invisible world and the structure of the entire universe. A master is someone who has resolved all the essential problems of life, who is free, who possesses an extremely strong will and who, above all else, is full of love, kindness, gentleness and light. What a tremendous amount of

* Following on the political events which are now common knowledge, the Bulgarian authorities commandeered the property of *Izgrev* as a site for foreign embassies, and forbade Peter Deunov's disciples to gather in the mountains at Rila for their summer camps. However, the Universal White Brotherhood, under the direction of the Master Omraam Mikhaël Aïvanhov, continued its activities in France; its headquarters at Sèvres, just outside Paris, is called *Izgrev*, after the headquarters of the Brotherhood in Bulgaria. For a few weeks each winter, the brothers and sisters gather at *Videlinata* (Monts de Corsier), in the mountains above Vevey in Switzerland and, during the summer holidays, at *The Bonfin,* near Fréjus, on the French Riviera. (Editor's note, March 1974)

work, and what concentrated study and perseverance it takes to become a master!

To be sure, one can say that everyone who teaches us something is a master for us and, in this sense, all men have one or more masters. In fact, in the west, lawyers, professors and even painters and writers are given the title of 'Master'. There is nothing wrong with that but, often enough, although such people have great talent and are very learned, many of them have not resolved the principal problems of their lives; they are not in control of their destiny, they do not know what direction to give their lives and they are often obliged to nourish the terrible desires and passions that possess and continually torment them. This is why they are not really masters in the initiatic sense of the word.

The power of a genuine master lies in the fact that all his actions are in perfect accord with his philosophy. He is the first to practise, in his own life, what he preaches to others; he is a living example. And to be a living example is to be a fountainhead, a spring to which plants, animals and human beings are drawn. This is why there are always disciples round a master. The Master Peter Deunov has forty thousand disciples in Bulgaria. In every town in the country there are groups of the Brotherhood, men and women who endeavour to live according to the rules of love, wisdom and truth.

Sometimes, listening to a recital by a great virtuoso, you are gripped by a profound emotion and feel that you would like to resemble him. And a painter or poet can inspire the same feelings. A true master, like an artist, has an extraordinarily powerful influence on the souls of others because, like a true poet who lives his poetry or a true musician who lives his music, a master lives the spiritual life.[5] He brings with him a world that can be sensed by all who come near him. To meet such a master is something truly precious, but to work to resemble him is far more precious still.

The greatest blessing a man can receive is to have a master to guide, direct and enlighten him. Unfortunately, though, people rarely listen to a master; how many masters in the past have already been burned at the stake or executed! And how many more have been forced to flee and leave the world to its sufferings!

Great misfortunes are raining down on humanity today, because it has always refused to listen to its spiritual masters; it has always despised and scoffed at them, and now it has no one to turn to, no one who could help it to overcome its difficulties.

A thousand years ago, Bulgaria saw the birth of Bogomilism, a very exalted spiritual teaching, which spread to most of the countries of Europe. The Bogomils were extremely pure, virtuous people and they were ready to be martyred and burned at the stake rather than give up living according to the teaching of the Gospels; among them were initiates and magi whom the masses respected and followed. But, from the beginning of time, those who shine more brightly than their fellows have always been an embarrassment to narrow-minded men who choose to live in obscurity, ignorance or greed, and the Bogomils were persecuted mercilessly. Many were killed, and others fled from Bulgaria and settled either in Italy or France, where they gave birth to other movements such as the Cathars and Albigensians, etc. Some of them settled in Germany and England, also, but it was principally in France that the spiritual movement born under the influence of the Bogomils flourished.

Bulgaria was cruelly punished for its crimes against the Bogomils: for five centuries its people were obliged to live under Turkish domination; thousands had their throats slit or were hanged, while thousands more were subjected to the most abject slavery.

Nowadays, there is hardly any religious persecution any more. But godly men and women inevitably arouse the animosity of those in high places because the purity of their lives makes their own cupidity, vanity and viciousness all the more obvious by comparison. Churches and governments are no longer free to commit injustices in this domain, but there are many individuals, often in very prominent positions in society, who misuse the power invested in them in virtue of their public office to protect their own private interests, even to the detriment of the interests of their country and their religion. Unfortunately, this kind of thing is not rare. Just as, in the past, the moral purity of the Albigensians highlighted, without their realizing it, the worldly motives of pope and clergy, so, today, the life of a genuine master shows up the all-too human attitude of certain Christians or priests who, while claiming to be heirs to the spiritual legacy of Christ, show less integrity than many atheists. This is why such masters inevitably find themselves a target for men bent on their destruction.

When the Master Peter Deunov first began his work in Bulgaria, this was the first obstacle in his path. He brought the teaching of the new life and showed men how far they were from the true teaching of Christ. Naturally, this did not please the bishops of the Orthodox Church, and they succeeded in getting the government to expel him from Sofia and exile him to Varna, which was where I lived. This was at the end of 1917.

For me, the Master's exile in Varna was the greatest good fortune and a decisive turning point in my life, for it was thanks to this that I came to know him. The Master remained in our town for several months and was soon the centre of a group of intelligent, very dedicated people who showed him great affection.

I cannot tell you all the details of our expeditions at sunrise, into the hills around Varna. You cannot imagine the beauty of the colours of those mornings, and the splendour of the sun as it rose over the Black Sea. How often the Master and I would sit there, just the two of us, caressed by the rays of the sun while we projected ourselves out of our bodies. He was my guide as I explored the other side and studied the realities of the invisible world. But these things are too precious and too intimate... it is not the moment to talk to you about them.

Several months after he had arrived in Varna, the Master was called back to Sofia. When men attack someone who is very pure, the evil aimed at him glances off the luminous shield of his aura and bounces back to strike those who gave birth to it. Psalm 91 says:

> '*A thousand may fall at your side,*
> *ten thousand at your right hand,*
> *but it will not come near you.*
> *You will only look with your eyes*
> *and see the punishment of the wicked.*
> *Because you have made the Lord your refuge,*
> *the Most High your dwelling-place,*
> *no evil shall befall you.*'

Naturally, this promise is valid only for someone who does the will of God, who loves God with all his heart, all his soul, all his thought and all his strength, one who is capable of sacrificing his whole life for the establishment of the kingdom of God on earth.

I know that you have all longed, at some point in your lives, to meet a master who will reveal truth to you; but you know, also, that this is extremely rare. In fact, some of you are probably convinced that all the great masters of the world are hidden away in Tibet, India, Japan, or even Africa, and that there are certainly none in Europe. We are very highly privileged in Bulgaria, therefore, to have the presence of such a highly revered Master. It is an immense joy to live with such a luminous being who is so full of love and kindness, and to be allowed to hear and see him in all the simplest details of everyday life. And what a joy to have a Master who can answer all the most obscure questions about the life of the soul[6] and the other worlds and their inhabitants,[7] who is able to explain how to communicate with the forces of nature[8] and the planetary spirits,[9] and who can also tell us how to preserve or recover our health through nutrition,[10] breathing exercises,[11] ablutions[12] and so on.

When the Master is at home, at *Izgrev* (this is where he lives, in the midst of the Brotherhood), his presence is immediately perceived. It is as though the very air vibrated differently. The brothers and sisters crowd round him and the hum of their voices can be heard a long way off. Every day, from morning to night, a constant stream of people comes to ask him for advice about their personal problems and, three times a week, he gives a lecture. The Master's way of speaking is astonishing. He never reads his lectures and he never quotes from well-known authors, as most lecturers do. He lets himself be guided by his inspiration and, as he can sense the worries and concerns of those who are listening to him, he helps them by speaking directly to their unspoken questions; many people leave the lecture, convinced that the Master was speaking just for them.

I have often taken friends to see the Master and, on the way to his house, we would talk about all kinds of different subjects. But, whatever we had been talking about, as soon as we arrived, the Master would pick up and continue the conversation at the point where we had left it. To their utter amazement, he would make some comment or question my friends about what they had just been saying. And this is something that happened not once or twice, but very, very often. All the Master's disciples know that he can read their thoughts. There is a French sister among you who went to Bulgaria to see the Master and she was astonished to find that he knew every detail of her life, who her friends were, here, in France, and so on. She was also very struck by the vitality and light that shone from his face. One day, she can tell you what she saw and learned in the Brotherhood in Bulgaria.

What is the difference between studying at a university and studying with a master? At university, a student learns things that are external to him, that are not an integral part of his life and, after several years of study, he finds himself exactly as he was before, with all the same vices and weaknesses. To be sure, he may have gained a reputation as a very knowledgeable, distinguished scholar, he may have learned to handle sophisticated instruments, to quote eminent authors, to use his tongue with considerable effect and, even, to make a lot of money, but his ability to deform the minds of other men will also have increased. Whereas he who has spent some years studying with a master, will, on the contrary, find himself profoundly transformed: his powers of discernment, his moral strength and his possibilities of action, both inward and outward, will have increased.

To study at university is comparable to making a scientific analysis of a fruit with the help of all the most up-to-date physical and chemical processes; you study in detail exactly what elements enter into the composition of the skin, pulp, pips and juice of that fruit, but you never taste it, you never examine it with the instruments that nature has put at your disposal, you never feel its effects in yourself. By contrast, a disciple who studies with a master learns nothing of all that, but he eats the fruit and, before long, discovers that all the wheels of his being – his brain, heart and will, etc. – have been set in motion, vivified and brought into harmony. With the help of these faculties, a disciple of such a master can venture into a study of the great book of nature in which he may see – far more clearly set out than in any university text – the physical, chemical and astronomical aspects of the universe, and learn how they are all interconnected.

Don't think that I am opposed to universities. I have been a student myself, for many years, and taken courses in several disciplines. After getting degrees in psychology and education, I studied mathematics, physics and chemistry; in fact, I used to be laughed at as 'the eternal student'! But I soon found out that I had been wasting a lot of time and I deliberately forgot much of what I had learned when I realized that it could be a screen between reality and my own life. It is useful to study certain disciplines; each one reveals an aspect of the universe and of life, but the point of view adopted in the universities today is such that only the inert, lifeless aspect of reality can be studied. One day, people will begin to realize that the sciences need to be vivified, by which I mean that they must be seen to apply to all aspects of nature. Then mathematical formulas and geometrical forms and properties will speak another language and we shall discover that the laws which govern our thoughts apply equally to our feelings and actions. This is what I mean when I speak of true science. At the moment, people know too much astronomy, anatomy or mathematics and they never see how these disciplines tie in together or how they tie in to life. All our knowledge is a collection of scattered, disconnected fragments; this is why it is of no practical use to us in life.

Try to understand what I am saying: I have nothing against knowledge or against those who dispense it, but the knowledge I am interested in is that which is dispensed by the great masters, for they are the only ones who understand the inestimable value of a science capable of bringing light, happiness and fulfilment to all men.

With the Master, I learned the art of listening to those who had something to teach me. If a piece of steel lies alongside a magnet for any length of time, it also becomes magnetized. In the same way, a disciple who is truly receptive towards his master is impregnated with his strength and magnetism and becomes capable of helping others. It is important to be receptive and constantly attentive to initiates, for the slightest indication on their part can warn us of future events. Unfortunately, their words often come back to us only after the events have taken place.

It is only in the Orient that people are truly receptive towards those who are superior to them. The disciples of an oriental master are totally open to his influence and instruction without fearing the loss of their individuality or freedom. It would never cross the mind of an Oriental to fear that he might become his master's slave. On the contrary, he is wholly convinced that it is only by being receptive to his Master that he will achieve his true individuality and independence.

When I say that a disciple must be receptive towards his master, I am not saying that he must confine this attitude of openness to initiates only; no, he must also be receptive towards the sun, springs, rivers, stars and the whole of nature... towards all that is noble and beautiful. This is the only way to learn to understand and get an inner sense of the work that these higher beings accomplish in the world that is invisible to us.

In almost all European countries, particularly in France, people think that by criticizing and looking down on everything and everyone, by adopting a supercilious attitude, as though they knew and understood everything, they show their true individuality. But the ways in which people in the West manifest their independence today simply shows that they are too lazy to make the effort to free themselves from their own shameful tendencies and too lacking in psychology to be capable of foreseeing the consequences of their acts.

It is true that there are very few masters in the West, because this widespread habit of publicly ridiculing all that is sacred has driven almost all of them away. The West is almost totally deprived of masters; in fact, if a few still remain, they are careful to hide from public view so as not to be disturbed. Most of those who call themselves masters are not only incapable of doing anything for anyone else, they do not even know how to get themselves out of the quagmire they are in.

People in the West put too much faith in the power of words; they are persuaded that endless talk can solve all their problems and they pay much less attention to actual achievements. A master also believes in the power of the word, but he does not say very much; he says only what is essential and his primary concern is to see that his actions match his words. The western world no longer lives in that deep inwardness that is the home of wisdom; it lives in the superficial, frivolous realm of interminable discourse!

Most of the people one meets are ready to talk a great deal on a purely external level, but they have nothing to say inwardly. Words pour from their lips, but not one of them reverberates in your soul, whereas most of what an initiate says is said inwardly; this is why, to the end of your life, you can never forget what they say to you.

Let me give you an example. Picture a student who is studying and becoming extremely knowledgeable under the direction of some very learned and renowned professors. Then, one day, he meets a young 'professor' who is not at all learned or renowned: a lovely, very pure young girl. The student immediately senses that she is saying something so delightful, profound and poetic, that he decides to enroll in her school and asks her to be his teacher. His learned professors at the university talked about literature, biology and astronomy, but their lessons left him unmoved and, for this reason, he was incapable of understanding their deeper underlying meaning. Even the most beautiful poetry failed to touch him, and now it is he who is writing poetry; he used to be bored to tears with astronomy, and today it is he who feels the need to contemplate the stars and compare their brilliance with the shining eyes of his new teacher. In spite of all he learned about hygiene, he would often be unwashed, unshaven and generally slovenly in appearance; and now, miracle of miracles, he is always spick and span, his tie carefully knotted, his cheeks smooth and clean-shaven, his clothes spotless! His family and friends cannot get over it! Before, he used to scoff at psychometry: he had no perception of the psychic dimension and despised those who claimed to be sensitive to it. But now, as soon as he receives the least little token from his young teacher (a brief note or a flower, for instance) he touches his eyes, his lips and his heart with it in the hope of picking up the subtle, mysterious waves that impregnate it. He has learned to feel the subtlest realities; the invisible world has become vitally real for him. In the past he would not believe in homoeopathy, but now he often experiences it for himself: his young teacher gives him only the most minute doses: a twinkle of the eye, a slight smile, a gentle handshake... and what powerful and marvellous effects they have on him!

The strange thing is that this young professor is a very skilled lawgiver. Her whole attitude teaches her pupil the first law of her school: 'Thou shalt have no other gods before me! Thou shalt love only me and shalt not cast your eyes on other young teachers of my kind!' Sometimes, his teacher becomes very demanding, but always with a view to furthering his studies! The student lives in the belief that he is a knight-errant whose mission is to release the princess from the clutches of the dragon – the girl's father, of course – who is trying to keep them apart!

If you are wondering why there are so many young lovers in the world, I can tell you that it is simply because older professors have exaggerated the importance of what they teach and their methods. When the watchful eye of nature looked at all the colleges, universities and seminaries full of professors, she was alarmed to see that, in the name of their very inadequate psychological and pedagogical science, they claimed the right to impose rules, laws and prescriptions which had no connection with her own laws or with the normal, reasonable conditions of life. So she sent young professors of both sexes to earth with the mission to lead each other to love and sacrifice.

Now, I am not saying that all these young professors are very wise. No, they are all apprentices and they do a lot of stupid things and make many mistakes, but that is not the point. On the other hand, I have no quarrel with old professors either. Symbolically, to be old means to be wise, and to be young means to be the child of love; youth and age are two poles, two expressions; one of love and the other of wisdom. When I use examples of this kind, I must ask you to try to understand me correctly.

Many people judge others on the basis of how much they know, and consider that the ability to stimulate others and communicate to them something of their own strength and courage in life is unimportant. But this is like despising bread, water and air. Neither philosophy nor science nor art are any good to anyone if he is not nourished and alive. What counts above all else, therefore, is to be nourished, to be alive, and only then, if one has the time and the inclination, to interest oneself in philosophy and science. At university, students are given a daily diet of philosophy and science but they are not nourished, and that is why (symbolically speaking) their legs tremble beneath them, their hearts are empty and their vision is blurred.[13] At the school of the great initiates it is just the opposite: the students are given plenty of nourishment and, once they are sufficiently strong and robust, they are taught how to plough the soil; then they are given a plough and set to work. The soil I am talking about is that which each man possesses within himself, in his own head. Those who know how to plant good seed in their own soil will never want for nourishment in their lives; the others will reap only thistles and thorns which will not only be of no use but will even be harmful to them and to others.

The professors in our universities have a detailed knowledge only of the outer dimension of man; they have forgotten to study the soil that God gave them. And they have never taken the trouble to sow good seed in it or to sow it in the right way or at the right season. But those who are wise study their own inner soil and cultivate it scientifically and, in this way, they are able to nourish all men with the fruits of their harvest. There is not much visible difference between these two kinds of professor, but what a tremendous difference in the results of their teaching! It is this slight difference that has led mankind to its present demonic way of life in which all men rob, deceive and assassinate their fellow men.

If you meet someone today who inspires you with a tremendous desire to live, if you feel full of hope and courage after talking to him, be sure that this is infinitely more worthwhile than if you had acquired some great philosophical knowledge, for, more often than not, that kind of knowledge leaves you empty and dried up. And in any case, when you are well disposed and full of love, joy and enthusiasm, knowledge will come to you of itself. I assure you that I would much rather spend my days with those who can give me an impetus, kindle in me a desire to work and teach me to love what I do, than with those who are as full of knowledge as an encyclopaedia but incapable of triggering my courage and enthusiasm.

Many people appreciate only those who are rich, well-informed and famous; they think that men and women who are full of love, kindness and tolerance, are stupid to be like that and that, if they were wise, they would adopt a different attitude. How wrong they are! If there were no kind, pure human beings, the world would have been destroyed a long time ago. It is thanks to such pure beings, thanks to the spiritual masters, that the world has survived; without them everything would disappear. When you associate with pure, noble, superior beings, you can feel that the forces surrounding them help and enlighten you. By contrast, when you associate with impure, unjust, evil human beings, you can sense that you are open and vulnerable to all kinds of negative influences. There is an old tradition that says that the grass never grows again where an evil person has trod. Yes, for destructive vibrations and forces emanate from the wicked. Nowadays, the worth of those who are kind, honest and full of virtue is not recognized; but the day will come when they will be appreciated.

Now I want to tell you of something that happened in Varna when I first knew the Master Peter Deunov and used to go and talk to him. It was during the Balkan war and I was seventeen years old. I often used to visit the Master, and when one is with him, one loses all notion of time. That particular evening, we had talked for a long time and it was late when I left him, long past the time imposed by curfew. In those days, the police patrolled the streets and arrested anyone who was out late and took them to the police station for the night. And I was very late. Suddenly, two mounted policemen appeared at the corner of the street, and arrested me, saying, 'Where are you going at this time of night?' 'I'm on my way home', I replied. 'Well, you'll begin by coming with us!' they said, and I was obliged to follow them. As I walked, I thought about the Master and the conversation we had had, and I was so happy that I really did not care that I had to spend the night in prison. But then, for no apparent reason, the guards' attitude changed and they said, 'Go on, go home! We'll go with you part of the way to see that you're not arrested by other guards, but don't go out again at this time of night!' Naturally, I was delighted at their change of attitude, but the next day I had forgotten the whole incident. A few days later, when I went back to see the Master, he received me with a smile, saying, 'How did it go the other evening? The guards were friendly, weren't they?' 'But Master', I exclaimed, 'How do you know what happened? What did you do?' And the Master replied, 'I told them that you were a good disciple and that they should let you go home in peace!' After this I understood how easy it was for a Master to speak in the invisible world. Those who wonder about the reality of thought, about whether it really can travel through space and influence human minds, would do well to think about these facts. The Master said to the guards, 'Let him go; he's a good disciple', and their souls heard and obeyed him, for the wishes of a master are commands.

Sometimes, when we were talking together, the Master would look up at the sky, at the patterns made by the clouds and say, for instance, 'Mikhaël', there are three people from Sofia coming to see me, this afternoon.' 'How can you see that?' I would ask him, and he would say, 'I can see it in the clouds; they have come to warn me in advance.' What language they spoke, I do not know, but, thanks to the Master, I learned a great deal about this question. He explained that the clouds hanging over a town could tell one about the quality of the souls who lived there. There are many signs in the invisible world which can be read and interpreted by initiates. When a town is full of impurities, noxious emanations hover over it and form a screen against all beneficial currents so that nothing but misfortune can reach it. The same phenomenon can be seen in the human aura: if someone is impure, his aura will be opaque and he will have to suffcr, because blessings from the divine world cannot reach him.

Every human being is accompanied by invisible entities, and if these entities are well-intentioned, they prepare the way for him wherever he goes, but if they are ill-intentioned, instead of facilitating things, they oppose and hinder him in everything he does. Someone who is truly a king is always preceded by servants who prepare his coming. By the time he arrives, everything is ready, simply because he is king. But a beggar, that is to say, someone who is poor in virtue, need not expect to receive a royal welcome when he goes somewhere. The secret of true life is to seek nothing else but to be king of oneself, a king in complete command of his thoughts, feelings and actions. Inside each one of us is an immense population which we must learn to govern. But I will talk to you about that another time.

A man who is truly in command of all his desires and tendencies is always preceded by beings who get things ready for him. If you fail to keep a watch on your thoughts and feelings, when you next undertake something, they will bring all your plans to nothing, because they will enter the minds of your friends and associates and work against you. Think about this for a while and you will understand that if you have adversaries it is you who have created them, it is you who have projected them around you and now they are working against you, through the brains of those in whom they have taken shelter. There are exceptions to this, of course. Human beings of a very high calibre, the great masters who spend their lives working for the evolution of mankind, are often opposed and persecuted by enemies, because the two principles of good and evil manifest themselves and are in constant combat with each other in the world. Those who work on the side of light know that they will inevitably arouse the forces of darkness. Their efforts to improve conditions in the world arouse the hostility of certain individuals by threatening their personal interests, and these people will go to any lengths to retaliate. As I have said, this is what happened with the Master Peter Deunov: the wisdom of his life, his disinterestedness and integrity endangered the interests of a great many people. The light is always feared by those who prefer the dark for, when it appears, they can be seen and recognized.

One day, one of my friends who was an actor and a fellow disciple, came to me in a great state of agitation. His voice trembled, as he said, 'Brother Mikhaël, a theatrical producer has come to Varna, and is planning to put on a play which attacks our Master. As you know, I belong to this theatre company, and that means that I'm going to have to take part in a play that ridicules the Master and the Brotherhood. What am I to do?' I told my friend, 'Don't worry. The invisible world is all-powerful; it will sort things out. But, if you can, go and talk to the producer and explain to him that he must not put on this play, that we have no right to ridicule men who are truly good, just and holy. Tell him that he doesn't know the laws: it is not an offence to laugh at criminals, in fact it can sometimes do good, but it is dangerous to laugh at pure, luminous beings.'

I was not at all worried; I was certain that this play would never be put on. The producer listened to what my friend had to say but refused to do as he asked and the rehearsals went on. Then came the day before opening night and the final rehearsal; all of a sudden, my friend came running to me, saying, 'Brother Mikhaël, you'll never guess what happened; the producer was struck down in the middle of rehearsal; an artery in his neck ruptured and the doctors are with him now, on the stage, trying to stop the haemorrhage.' I reassured him and told him that it was not serious, and asked him to tell the producer that I would like to talk to him. The man agreed to see me and, when I got there, I asked to speak to him alone. This did not please his wife at all, but she ended by allowing me to see him alone. When I went into his room, I looked at him kindly; I could see that he was in a panic. He lay there, motionless, with a bag of ice on his throat, unable to talk; he could do no more than look at me. Very peacefully and lovingly, I said, 'You can be cured, but on condition that you promise me not to put on that play. There are a lot of other plays to choose from; why try to make money with this one? If you put it on you will be working against those who bring something pure and luminous to the world, and you have no right to do that. It is because you are trying to do this that you are ill.' Then I explained some of the laws of the invisible world and the danger in which he stood. As he was very weak, he was more receptive than usual and he understood and promised not to put on the play. I left him, well content, and the very next day he was cured. But a few days later, his wife (who was an actress and had a part in the play) started to jeer at him and told him that he had been stupid to promise not to put it on, and that his cure had nothing to do with his promise. He let himself be convinced and decided to begin rehearsing again but, at the very first rehearsal, he was, once again, struck down by the same thing... This time he really understood and gave up any idea of producing the play. The inhabitants of Varna never did have the pleasure of seeing it!

At one time I was living with a friend of mine and, when I got home one day, he told me that a thief had broken in while we were out and stolen a lot of our belongings, among which were a radio and a watch that belonged to me. I thought about it for a moment and then I said, 'Don't worry. If those things truly belong to us, we'll get them back.' I had heard the Master explain that when something was stolen, it often meant that it did not really belong to us and that, in a previous life, we had injured the thief in some way: either we had stolen something of his or prevented him from acquiring it. But, of course, it can happen that a thief makes a mistake and takes things which he believes belong to him whereas, in fact, they don't. If that is the case, the policemen of the invisible world who put all these things to rights, can get our belongings back for us; but if they really do belong to the thief, we never get them back. This is why I told my friend that if those things were really ours, we would get them back but that, if we did not get them back, it would mean that they did not belong to us, so we should not shed any tears over them! My friend was very intelligent but, above all, he was very practical and was not at all amused. He thought it would be much better to report the theft to the police station, and that is what he did, giving both our names. Two days later, I was summoned to an interview with the commissioner of police. When I went into his office, the commissioner said, 'You're a disciple of the Master Peter Deunov, aren't you?' 'Yes', I replied; 'But how can you tell?' 'I can see it in your face' said the commissioner. 'Do you know the Master?' I asked him. 'Yes; I know him and I'll tell you how it happened', replied the officer and, forgetting all about the thief, he began: 'How fortunate you are to have such a Master! What makes me say that? I'll tell you. During the war I was at the front, in Macedonia, and my father was governor of Varna. It was extremely difficult to get letters from home or for our letters to reach our families, in those days, and my father was worried at being without news of me. Hearing that your Master was in Varna, he went to see him and asked him if he could find out where I was. The Master closed his eyes for a moment, looking for me; then he said, "At the moment, your son is in a forest with his comrades. They are hiding because there are enemy planes over the forest, dropping bombs; they are afraid, because the place is very exposed. There is a stream nearby, also. Now a bomb has just fallen where they are hiding... Your son is wounded, but not fatally. He will be safe, so don't worry. I can assure you that he will not die and that he will soon be back in Varna. Go to the station to meet him (and the Master told him exactly the date and time he should be there), and he will arrive, bringing a fish with him." My father was very moved. On the day mentioned by the Master, he went to the station with his friends, and was overjoyed when, sure enough, I arrived. Later, my father took me to see the Master and asked him to study my head (he was a first-class phrenologist), but I don't remember much of what he told me; I didn't take anything very seriously at the time and was quite incapable of understanding what your Master was saying.'

After telling me his story, the commissioner questioned me about the theft and promised to do what he could to find the thief, and I went home. The thing I really wanted to get back was my watch, and I'll tell you why. It was a silver watch and it was at least fifty years old (it had been my father's), but its value came from the fact that I had marked on it the planetary influence for each hour of the day. I had worked out this astrological dial after doing all the appropriate calculations, and now I only had to glance at my watch to know the planetary influence at any given moment. That was why I was anxious to get it back. And I did. The thief was a young man who was very poor. I tried to talk to him in the hopes of touching his heart, and then I asked the commissioner not to be too hard on him, reminding him that he was the victim of social conditions, that he was poor and hungry. He did not seem to find my arguments very convincing, but at least he promised not to ill-treat him. When I got home that day, I told my friend, 'You see? The invisible police force does its work very well. It discovered that the theft was a mistake!' He hugged me with joy, because it was he who had lost the most.

One day, in Sofia, I met a well-known author who wrote extremely well. He said, 'Tell me about your Master. He must be getting old, now; what is he doing? When I was still at school, a friend and I went to see him; we had heard that he was a very good phrenologist and we wanted him to foretell our future. He smiled at us and, to me, he said, 'Your health is not very good, but you will become a distinguished writer.' I was very surprised because, at the time, I wanted to go in for commerce; I didn't have the slightest desire to write. But my friend, who did want to become a writer, was very disgruntled when your Master told him that he would go into business! Later, everything happened exactly as he had said it would. Please convey my respects to your Master; I have a very high opinion of him.'

When we were at the camp, up in the mountains near the seven lakes of Rila, the Master would give us certain exercises to do. I cannot describe them all, but I want to tell you about one of them, which may seem very bizarre and quite incomprehensible if you don't know certain laws of Initiatic Science. The Master would say, 'Go and get some water from the lake and pour it over the rocks near the edge of the lake. Do this ten times running.' Off we would go, full of joy, to do what he had told us, because we knew that whatever task he gave us it was always useful and meaningful.

Every human being has ties with the different kingdoms of nature and particularly with the mineral kingdom, although only the initiates can discern these ties. The stones or plants to which we are connected may be as far away as America or Australia, but if someone moves or damages them or cuts them down, we feel the hurt. And the same is true for animals: when we slaughter them for food, we are injuring, without realizing it, all those with whom they have ties. So much so, in fact, that we can actually cause their death. I had a friend in Bulgaria who had a magnificent garden full of a great variety of plants and fruit trees. One day, he wanted to build a house there, so he decided to cut down a group of trees to make room for it. But one of his friends was extremely attached to a pear tree which produced magnificent fruit but which was destined to be cut down. His affection for that tree was quite extraordinary, although he had no idea why. When he heard that his friend was planning to cut down the tree he loved, he begged him not to do it, but to no avail; the pear tree was cut down with all the others. Very shortly after, this friend fell seriously ill and died.

I wish I had time to give you more examples, for there are a great many of them. As for the exercise the Master had given us to do, I am sure that when we poured the water from the lake over the rocks, it enabled those who had ties with these rocks to receive help, without knowing where it came from. Perhaps, at that moment, they felt refreshed and healed. I think so, for these laws are real. I am simply opening a little window for you, here, but I invite you to think about the bonds that exist between us and the different kingdoms of nature.

In the Brotherhood in Sofia, there was a Belgian sister who had a very large dog. When it barked, it made everybody tremble, although, actually, it wasn't savage... it was simply rather surprising! One day, the Master said, 'Look at that dog, the person who has a special connection with it used to be a black magician in Atlantis and he did a great deal of harm. This shows you that the laws are implacable: that black magician is now obliged to live in a dog.' Some of the brothers wanted to see if they could prove this, so they drew magic signs on the ground in front of the dog and, sure enough, it reacted in the most extraordinary way, as though it were trying to manifest powers it had possessed in the past.

Since we are talking about these things, I want to tell you about another, really extraordinary incident that I cannot explain. One year, we were up in the Rila mountains, with a friend who was a musician. I had my violin with me as well and, on a fine night, we would sing and play the violin together. One evening we were beside a very beautiful little lake and my friend played a lovely serenade: *The legend of Veniaski.* We were soon joined by a good many tourists, attracted no doubt, by the sound of the violin. Some of them sat down on the grass and talked to us while many more went and washed their feet in the lake. This was something my friends and I never did; morning and evening we would take water from the lake and then go and wash on the grass. Very pure and sensitive beings of a very high order live in mountain lakes and we can upset them dreadfully if we behave thoughtlessly towards them. They only accept disciples who understand and respect the fact that nature is alive. So, as

I was saying, while we were talking to some of these tourists, others were washing their feet in the lake. Then, after a time, they all went away again.

But the next day, when my friend and I went back to the lake, it had disappeared! Yes, there was no more lake, only a stretch of dry, stony ground. We rubbed our eyes again and again in complete bewilderment, and went down into what had once been the lake to see if we could find a hole or a crack in the ground through which the water could have drained away. But we found nothing of the kind, and the ground looked as though it had been dry for months! What had happened? We stayed there a long time, puzzling over the problem and only one answer seemed possible: the impurity or evil emanations of some of the tourists who had bathed in the lake the evening before had caused it to disappear. Some invisible nature spirits had come and taken it away. You will object that that is ridiculous, that such an explanation is totally impossible from a scientific point of view. Perhaps, but science has not studied everything; there are still a great many things it knows nothing about and a great many more that it is incapable of interpreting. And believe me, I am inventing nothing. As I am speaking to you I am also speaking in the presence of the invisible world, which knows very well that what I say is true. As for my interpretation of this phenomenon, nothing obliges you to accept it, but one thing is certainly true, and that is that it is possible for nature to be greatly disturbed by the wickedness of man. You have all read tales that tell of beings so evil that, wherever they went, plants, animals and even human beings sickened and died. The normal course of life ceased in their presence and desolation and disaster reigned. It is not only in legends that such beings exist; they can still be found in the world, today, and it is the greatest possible curse for any family, society or nation to be obliged to nurture the bearers of such baneful forces.

A few years ago the newspapers were full of the case of an opera singer who had extraordinary power in his glance. He was one of the best singers in Europe and he was singing in the role of a man who was supposed to curse his mistress. At the first performance, he played his part with such conviction and ardour that when he cursed the prima donna who was playing the part of his mistress, the look he gave her caused her to fall to the ground, unconscious. When they picked her up, she was dead! The singer had a feeling that there might be some connection between the curse and the woman's death, so the following night, instead of looking at the person he was cursing, he decided to look up at the ceiling. But this time, when he uttered his curse, the dead body of a stagehand fell into the midst of the actors on the stage; the singer's glance had reached him and struck him down where he had been working, up in the flies. Once again the opera was interrupted in the midst of a commotion that you can well imagine. No one but the wretched singer connected these accidents with the curse that he had uttered, but on the following evening, realizing what was happening, he decided to look at a box to one side of the stage which, he knew, would be unoccupied all evening. This time, the opera went off without a hitch. After it was all over, however, they found the body of a countess, crumpled up on the floor of the box: arriving after the curtain had gone up, she had slipped in to the empty box so as not to disturb anyone. Dismayed by so many fatal accidents, the director of the opera house refused to allow that opera to be put on again.[14]

The Master told us that, one day, in the United States, he had seen a demonstration of the extraordinary magnetic power of a young girl. Several people held a heavy wooden beam which twisted as the girl brushed it with her hand. When she repeated the gesture a second time, the beam broke into little pieces!

There are all kinds of little things that reveal, less spectacularly, no doubt, the invisible influence that people can exert on their surroundings. If bees find themselves in the immediate vicinity of thieves and criminals, for instance, they will leave their hive. They are extremely sensitive to the emanations of perverse human beings, so they get as far away from them as possible. This would be a good field of research for scientists of the future: to find out how such tiny insects can distinguish thieves and scoundrels from honest men.

But let me tell you one more anecdote. A very long time ago, we went with a friend, to spend some time by a lake called the Altar. We stayed on the shores of this lake for three weeks, meditating, studying, playing the violin and singing. The Master had told us that very highly evolved beings lived up in the mountains and that if human beings destroyed the purity of their environment it upset them very much. For this reason we were very careful to keep a guard on our thoughts and feelings and our attitude in general. We had already spent three weeks up there, in magnificent weather, and this, in itself, was a real miracle, because the weather is always extremely changeable up among those peaks. After three weeks, clouds began piling up and the sky grew darker and darker. The whole of nature seemed to be saying to us: 'That's enough. You must go now; we have other work to do.' We had no tent and the rain was already beginning, when it occurred to us that we might say a few words to the spirits of nature and see if they would grant our request. So we said, 'You, who are our friends, hear us! We're not ready to leave; give us the time to get our baggage ready.' To our amazement, the rain stopped immediately. We collected all the gear we had brought with us, our knapsacks were soon buckled up and we were ready to leave, but we were so pleased with the lull that we had been granted, that we thought to ourselves: 'Perhaps it won't rain, after all. It was only a few drops. Perhaps we can stay longer...' We had barely had time to formulate this thought when the rain came down again with extraordinary violence. Of course, we left immediately, but it was very cold and we had to walk through the storm for six hours. Nature is full of good, intelligent and powerful beings and they were punishing us for wanting to stay in spite of the warning they had given us. You are free to think what you like about this story.

The influence people can have on each other or on inanimate objects can manifest itself in various ways. You might have a friend, for instance, who is very pure and innocent, as limpid as a mountain lake, and you throw your impurities into him... In other words, you wash your feet in the pure water of this lake. Very few people stop to think before acting. A high degree of inner advancement is necessary to prevent us from throwing ourselves avidly and greedily at a very pure, beautiful soul! No wonder people are so afflicted by disappointments, separations and regrets. Very few people are capable of respecting a beautiful soul so as to continue to receive the inspiration and impetus it could give them, every day, so as to continue to have occasion to rejoice and to create. And yet the reward for protecting a soul is a thousand times greater than anything that is to be gained by hastening to defile and destroy it. So many tragedies are caused by a lack of understanding of this question.

Beauty and purity can make us happy; they can even bring us back to life if we know how to contemplate them without soiling them. Human beings are mistaken when they think that the world of beauty is something that can be possessed. No one has ever been able to grasp beauty; as soon as one approaches and tries to touch it, it slips away and disappears.[15] Beauty is a world that has been created exclusively for the eyes; it is destined neither for the mouth nor for the hands. Beauty likes to be looked at but without being touched.

Blessed are those who can understand and apply these important rules about beauty, for joy, happiness and peace depend on the respect one has for beauty and purity. Another time I will explain what you need to know about measure, distance, dosage and proportions. We must be very attentive to beings that are beautiful and pure, for our attitude can drive away the entities that dwell in them and, when they go, we suffer as well, and all inspiration disappears. He who contemplates beauty every day sings and lives.

I have a friend in Bulgaria who is a professor and a historian. He is a very sincere person and, one day, he said, 'You know, Brother Mikhaël, there's something I'd like to tell you. It is something very precious that I have kept to myself for a long time, but now I'd like to share it with you. As you know, I once had a wife and son and I was very rich, but then I lost everything. For years, my life was one long succession of tribulations which caused me a great deal of suffering; I could not understand why destiny pursued me so relentlessly. One day, I was walking in the forest near Izgrev; I was feeling particularly miserable that day, and there, hidden among the trees, I started to cry. Suddenly, I heard footsteps coming through the woods, behind me. I didn't want anyone to see me in such a state, but when I turned round it was the Master. He was coming towards me, quite quietly, and it was obvious that he knew that I was there. 'What are you doing here?' he asked; 'What's the matter?' 'Oh, Master', I exclaimed; 'I cannot help crying... I have suffered so much!' But the Master smiled at me and said, 'Yes, I know. But don't distress yourself; everything's going to be all right. Do you remember how much you suffered when you lost such-and-such a thing?' 'Yes.' 'And how, afterwards, you understood such-and-such a law?' 'Yes, Master; I remember.' 'And do you remember how much you suffered, again, when you lost such-and-such?' 'Yes.' 'And it was after that, wasn't it, that you understood such-and-such a law?' 'Yes, Master. You're right.' 'Well', continued the Master; 'Now I can tell you that it was I who sent you those trials.' The astonishing thing was that the events the Master had mentioned had happened years before my friend had even heard of him, and only he and his late wife had known about them.

And then the Master explained. He said, 'Have you understood what I am saying? I'll tell you why I sent you those trials. It was because you still had a very heavy karmic debt to pay and you could never have understood the great mysteries of life if you did not pay it. So, in order to help you to evolve more rapidly, I changed something in your destiny. But from now on you can be at peace; everything will be all right.'

It would take too long to explain all the cases in which great masters are entitled to intervene in the course of our lives. In the normal way, they don't do so; they respect the laws of destiny. If they intervene, it is for reasons which are beyond our powers of comprehension. We cannot avoid paying our debts; we can do so more quickly or more slowly, but we have to pay them. But we must realize that, in order to evolve more rapidly, it is better to get rid of certain debts as quickly as possible, and it is in cases like this that, from time to time, a master will intervene. It sometimes happens, therefore, that a master intervenes in the destiny of certain disciples in order to release them from the grip of circumstances which, like the gangue concealing a precious stone, prevent the truth, wisdom and love buried deep within them from rising to the surface. But a disciple has to earn this privilege by sincerely seeking the light. A master will not change everyone's destiny; he will only do it for those who really deserve it, otherwise it would not even be of any use to them. If our hearts are dead and our minds in darkness, we can never change, even with the help of a master.

Many years ago, when I was still very young, the Master asked me to climb Mount Musala (3,000 metres), at night. This meant that I had to go through a forest in which bears, wild boar and wolves lurked, and where it was almost impossible to see one's way at night. Not only that, but I had to choose a dark night without a moon, and the fir trees in that forest are very tall and grow very close together. I had often climbed the Musala by day, but at night, in such conditions, I wondered how I would manage not to lose my way. The Master had said, 'The experience will help you to understand a great many things.' Yes, because we only really and truly understand something when we actually put it into practice and find ourselves without any outside support. Sometimes the invisible world leaves us with nothing, with no external support or purchase, because this forces us to find it within ourselves: in God.[16] When this is the case, the higher psychic forces within us increase for, when we have faith in the invisible realities, our spiritual potential is strengthened.

As the Master had asked, therefore, I waited for a moonless night, took some provisions for the road and a stick – not to defend myself against bears; it would have been useless, but to help me on my way – and off I went. You can certainly understand what I felt when I found myself in the forest. It was not fear, for I had already had so many amazing experiences with the Master that I was certain that he would be by my side to help me. If I had not had this conviction I would never have undertaken such an adventure. The thing that most struck me was the silence and the darkness. Even if someone had walked beside me I could not have seen him! The path ran alongside a ravine and there was nothing to protect me from a fall; how could I hope to stay on it? I groped my way along in that inky darkness, my imagination conjuring up pictures of wild boar and bears and every kind of danger! Then, at one point, I stopped and began to pray. I can assure you, in moments such as that, one prays with fervour; I could feel that I had never prayed like that before! And then, only a few moments after that ardent prayer, I saw a light which lit up the path for about two yards ahead of me and, from then on, I went on my way, singing and filled with joy, and I could feel a movement within me as though new currents were flowing through me.

After walking for several hours, I suddenly heard the baying of dogs. I could tell from the sound that it came from two of the great hounds that one sometimes comes across in the forests of Bulgaria, and which can easily attack and kill a man. I stopped and thought to myself, 'Two dogs! What does that mean? What should I do? Turn round and go back? No, they would only come after me and I can't hope to defend myself with my stick. There's only one thing for it: I must keep walking towards them.' I could hear them coming nearer and, from their bark, I could tell that they had picked up my scent and were hunting for me. I learned, later, that they were guard dogs from a sawmill in the forest, not far from there. I linked myself, in my mind, to the invisible world, to the brothers of the White Brotherhood, to the Master, to light, and started to walk quickly towards the dogs, feeling quite confident that the light would protect me. I sensed that this was going to be a decisive moment. It was almost daybreak and the hounds were soon close enough to see me; they raced towards me, barking furiously. Two or three yards from me, they paused and prepared to attack. One of them was white and the other grey and both were the size of a small donkey! Everything that followed happened very quickly, much more quickly than it takes to tell! Their jaws were wide open and threatening and they were ready to leap at me but I, feeling myself to be full of light and faith, thrust out my right hand towards them in a tremendously strong gesture. It was a moment of exceptional gravity; I could sense the presence of invisible entities and of the Master, and what I witnessed then, would have been enough to prove that the divine world existed, even if I had never received any other proof, before or since. As I threw my hand in their direction, both dogs gave out a frightful, rending howl and were picked up by some invisible force and literally thrown to the ground several yards from me, and there they crouched, motionless and silent, without looking at me, in an attitude that spoke of their terror.

I paused to get my breath back and, feeling completely without fear, I spoke to the dogs, saying, 'I'm very sorry to have given you such a shock, but you should have seen that I was a disciple and not tried to attack me and stop me from passing.' When I saw that they still did not move and were not going to try to hurt me, I felt an immense joy and, standing beside them, I spent a few minutes in thankful prayer to heaven. You must realize that a disciple has the right to use light in his own defence. If his adversary refuses the light that is aimed at him and which is intended to enlighten him, the pure, divine nature of that light causes the evil in his heart to be turned against him.

After a few minutes rest, standing by the dogs, I felt a great tiredness as though all my strength had been drained from me. Painfully, I started on my way again, then I sat down on a stone, completely exhausted, to pray and thank the entities of the invisible world for helping me; then, very slowly, I started off again and, after walking for several more hours I reached the top of Mount Musala just as the sun was rising. Oh, how grateful I was and how I thanked God when I saw the sun!

That experience taught me that a great many of the trials and tribulations of life are sent by the invisible world with the purpose of teaching us to rely on our inner spiritual strength. When we are well-fed, rich and prosperous, we remain at the surface of things whereas, in solitude and sorrow, we begin to rely on the Supreme Being dwelling within us. This was what all the ancient initiations were for: to teach man to turn inwards in search of the only true wealth, strength and security that dwell within him. In the old days, Initiation was always given in the temples; nowadays it is given at any time and in any place, in the everyday things of life when one is least expecting it. But every one of us will have to pass through earth, water, air and fire.

I sense that you are thinking, 'But why doesn't the invisible world warn us in advance of the trials we are going to have to endure?' Precisely because, when they come unexpectedly, we are obliged to dig deeper into ourselves and to make greater efforts. You should all rejoice because you are all going to have to endure trials! In the initiations of Antiquity, the fire that the candidates had to go through was actually an artificial brazier, but they did not know this; they thought that it was real. If they were afraid, it meant that they were unfit for initiation and they were sent away; but those who were daring and courageous and full of faith passed through the fire and discovered only afterwards that it was an illusion. All the trials we meet with in life are imaginary. Before having to endure them, we think, 'How awful... I am bound to suffer atrociously.' But if we accept them as we should, they don't seem quite so difficult. If your life is full of trials, therefore, you should be glad of it.

Before I conclude, I want to tell you a story. Once upon a time there was a king who went to stroll through the market (this is the kind of thing that happens in stories!). He was watching the merchants selling their different wares when, all of a sudden, he heard one of them crying out, 'Wisdom, wisdom. Who wants to buy some wisdom? Wisdom for sale!' The king, very astonished, went up to him and asked, 'Are you really selling wisdom? How much can you let me have?' 'One hundred, one thousand or ten thousand crowns worth.' replied the merchant. 'I'll take ten thousand crowns worth!' said the king. 'Right', said the merchant: 'Here you are: "Do what you have to do, but think of the consequences!"' The king was rather surprised at having to pay so much for a piece of advice which seemed so elementary, but he took it as a good joke, and went back to the palace, repeating the phrase to himself. The next day, he amused himself by repeating: 'Do what you have to do, but think of the consequences'. The time came for his barber to come and shave him; the man came in as usual, set out his equipment, and was just picking up the razor, when the king thought of the wisdom he had bought in the market and jokingly assuming a grave, stentorian voice, said, 'Do what you have to do, but think of the consequences'. To his stupefaction, the barber fell to his knees, crying, 'Oh, sire, forgive me! Forgive me! I didn't want to do it. It was your ministers who told me to cut your throat!' The king did his best to conceal his surprise and to look as though he knew all about it. Then the barber told him the whole story, and the king punished his treacherous ministers. If he had not bought ten thousand crowns worth of wisdom, he would have had his throat slit!

Sometimes, one simple thought, if it is that of a sage or master, can do more to save us than all the scientific knowledge in the world. We have to know which thoughts can save us and which can damn us. Every day, inside each one of us, is a barber, sent by ministers who are plotting our downfall. Already, we are no longer kings: our passions have dethroned us and are plotting to destroy us. If we are not protected, if we do not constantly repeat words of wisdom to ourselves, we shall have our throats well and truly cut. But if we keep murmuring profound, wise formulas in our hearts, those who approach with the intention of killing us will not dare to act.

I don't have time, this evening, to tell you more about the Master who has sent me to bring his teaching to France, but think about all that I have said today, and many things will become clear to you.

Paris, 12 March 1938

Notes

1. See Peter Deunov: *'Paneurythmie'* (Paroles et Musique); Muriel Urech: *'La paneurythmie de Peter Deunov à la lumière de l'enseignement d'Omraam Mikhaël Aïvanhov'; CD Paneurythmie.*
2. See *The Path of Silence,* Izvor Coll. n° 229, chap. 13: 'The Revelations of a Starry Sky'.
3. See *What is a Spiritual Master?,* Izvor Coll. n° 207.
4. See *La pédagogie initiatique,* Complete Works, vol. 27, chap. 3: 'Education et instruction. La puissance de l'exemple'.
5. See *Creation: Artistic and Spiritual,* Izvor Coll. n° 223.
6. See *Langage symbolique, langage de la nature,* Complete Works, vol. 8, chap. 1: 'L'âme', and chap. 2: 'L'être humain et ses différentes âmes'.
7. See *Angels and other Mysteries of The Tree of Life,* Izvor Coll. n° 236.
8. See *The Fruits of The Tree of Life – The Cabbalistic Tradition,* Complete Works, vol. 32, chap. 7: 'The Four Elements', chap. 8: 'Evening Vigils Round the Fire', etc., *The Mysteries of Fire and Water,* Izvor n° 232, chap. 3: 'Water, the Matrix of Life', chap. 5: 'The Living Chain of Sun, Earth and Water', chap. 8: 'Physical and Spiritual Water', and chap. 10: 'The Essential Role of Fire'.
9. See *The Fruits of The Tree of Life – The Cabbalistic Tradition,* Complete Works, vol. 32, chap. 4: 'The Tetragrammaton and the Seventy-Two Planetary Spirits'.

10. See *The Yoga of Nutrition,* Izvor Coll. n° 204.
11. See *Respiration – Spiritual Dimensions and Practical Applications,* Brochure n° 303.
12. See *The Mysteries of Yesod – Foundations of the Spiritual Life,* Complete Works, vol. 7, Part IV, chap. 3: 'Washing', and chap. 4: 'The Real Baptism'.
13. See *Youth: Creators of the Future,* Izvor Coll. n° 233, chap. 6: 'Knowledge Cannot Give Meaning to Life', and chap. 7: 'Character Counts for More than Knowledge'.
14. See *The Book of Divine Magic,* Izvor Coll. n° 226, chap. 13: 'The Power of a Glance'.
15. See *'Know Thyself' – Jnana Yoga,* Complete Works, vol. 18, chap. 1: 'Beauty'.
16. See *The Wellsprings of Eternal Joy,* Izvor Coll. no 242, chap. 4: 'Seeking God's answers within'.

Chapter Eight

THE LIVING CHAIN OF THE
UNIVERSAL WHITE BROTHERHOOD

All creatures, of all the different realms of nature, are linked to each other. Without our realizing it, we have ties to all beings on both the higher and the lower planes of creation. Initiates, who have studied this question, tell us that the knowledge of this link between the different realms of creation can be a great help to us in our spiritual life, principally because all the successes and failures, sufferings and joys of our everyday lives become so much clearer and more comprehensible when we know how and with whom we are linked.

If you live on the eighth floor of a building, you can go up and down in the lift. All you have to do is get into the lift and press a button and it will take you where you want to go. And look at how children climb trees, and how aircraft fly high up in the sky. There is no phenomenon in the visible world that does not correspond to an equivalent phenomenon in the spiritual world. Every single thing that exists on the physical plane, every object, every invention or construction, every profession, corresponds to something that exists in the spiritual world. Our consciousness can go up or down, exactly like a lift but, often enough, we don't know which button to push to make it go the way we want it to. Sometimes, without realizing it, we push the button for hell and drop straight down; sometimes we find ourselves in heaven, still without knowing exactly what we did to get there.

Only the initiates know which button to press to go to heaven consciously.

One of the marvels of Paris is the metro. At certain stations, as you know, there are moving staircases which are set in motion by a device which consists of a narrow beam of light from one side of the mouth of the escalator which strikes a light-sensitive cell on the opposite side. When a passenger crosses the path of the beam and breaks the contact, the photoelectric cell activates the machinery and the staircase starts moving. And we have exactly the same kind of mechanisms in us: although we don't know it, our hearts, minds and nervous systems obey the very same laws. Sometimes we emit terrible thoughts, feelings and words and it never occurs to us to wonder what will be set in motion by them and with what results. In fact, we often do things without making any attempt to foresee the consequences!

The truth is that there is a science which enables those who possess it to gauge the importance of their thoughts and feelings, to know what influence they will exert and the effects they will produce, etc. So far, this science is virtually unknown, but it is destined to be the science of the future. Without it, man will never really evolve: he will be raised to great heights, dropped to the depths and swung to and fro by events and circumstances over which he has no control, and he will never know what it is to be happy. Human beings have studied every imaginable science, but this, the most important of all, they have neglected. They perform miracles on the physical plane, but they are abysmally ignorant of everything that concerns the inner life! The science I am talking about reveals the reactions that take place in man's physical, chemical and mechanical dimensions as a result of his thoughts, feelings and actions, depending on whether they are good or bad. It teaches that a person's thoughts and feelings affect very subtle glands and organs in his body (which are like so many switches on the physical plane) and cause them to secrete substances that can be either beneficial or detrimental to him when they enter the blood stream. Our thoughts and feelings, therefore, trigger certain mechanisms within us and, depending on their nature, we are either enlightened or plunged into darkness, strengthened or weakened, liberated or imprisoned. The glands in question, tiny though they may be, hold the keys to all our inner forces. Picture a man who is planning to steal some money from his neighbour. To begin with, the plan is no more than a thought in his mind, but that thought is already at work: it has broken the contact between the beam of light and the photoelectric cell and the gears of the escalator are beginning to move. Or take the case of a man who is beginning to be interested in a woman in a certain way: whether consciously or unconsciously, he sets in motion certain physiological processes. Or again, imagine that you are preparing to suck a lemon: a process of secretion is immediately set in motion in your salivary glands. A thought may have an almost negligible effect outwardly, therefore, but it can be extremely potent inwardly.[1]

And then there is doubt: have you ever observed the effects of doubt? If you allow yourself to be overcome by doubt, it will chill and strangle and paralyse your soul.[2] Doubt affects certain glands and the glands secrete substances which, when they are injected into the bloodstream, cause life to shrink and shrivel up, both inwardly and outwardly. Children sometimes amuse themselves by floating celluloid fish in a bowl of water. On one end of each fish is a little block of camphor which makes the fish swim, but if you put even the tiniest drop of oil onto the surface of the water, the fish immediately stop moving. Well, we are like those celluloid fish: doubt has exactly the same effect on us as the oil has on them. We are often motivated by a noble impulse, by the desire to do God's will, to live a life of wisdom, and then, insidiously, doubts creep in and, like that drop of oil, put a stop to those impulses. As a matter of fact, doubt is not the only thing that has this effect; there are all kinds of thoughts and feelings that can paralyse people: fear, distrust, hostility, hatred, and so on. But then there are others, such as joy, faith, hope, love and enthusiasm which, on the contrary, give us a sense of

inner freedom and expansion. They can even change things for
the better on a physiological level. If you really want to dry up
completely and live in a strait-jacket, you only have to cultivate
thoughts of fear, hostility and doubt. As a matter of fact, quite a
lot of people seem to enjoy such thoughts: they even invent new
ones every day. Yes, they open all their doors and windows and
invite them in! But no initiate would ever entertain thoughts of
this nature; it is enough for them to know that they exist. Even
from a distance, they have no difficulty in recognizing them, for
their forms and colours are quite distinctive!

My dear brothers and sisters, from now on you must give
up whatever arrests your upward impetus; you must ally
yourselves with love, hope, beauty, faith, inspiration and all that
is capable of stimulating you, of filling you with the breath of
true life and enabling you to act with real freedom. All these
inner transformations imply the application of a vast science. I
cannot explain, today, the relationship between this science and
astrology, but I shall do so another time.

At the moment, I simply want you to understand that man
enjoys a permanent relationship with every other being in
creation, whether of a higher or a lower order. There is a living
hierarchy in nature which links all creatures in one unbroken
chain, and it is thanks to this hierarchy and to our ties with beings
of a higher order that we have the power to climb to greater
heights. But it is also by means of this hierarchy that we are
linked to all creatures of a lower order, even to the very stones
of the earth. Yes, the bond that binds man to animals, plants
and rocks is extremely powerful.* It is possible, for instance, to
help certain beings simply by pouring water over the stones with
which they have a special bond. If we cut down a tree here, in
France, we may be affecting someone who lives very far away,
perhaps on another continent, and that person may fall ill or
experience a feeling of distress without understanding the cause.

* See the references to this in the previous chapter.

And the same applies to animals: we kill animals, but nature is a living organism, and when we kill an animal it is as though we killed or injured certain glands in that organism: the equilibrium of the whole is disrupted and, before long, war breaks out between human beings. Yes, simply because they have butchered and eaten millions of animals! People have never realized that, because of the relationship between animals and men, when they kill animals they are also condemning men to death.[3] And yet, that is exactly what they are doing. You will say that it is because they are ignorant. Yes, you are probably right. But why are men so ignorant? Why do they want to remain ignorant? Everybody keeps saying that we simply must achieve peace in the world, that there must be no more war. But war will always be with us as long as we continue to slaughter animals because, in killing them, we are killing something in ourselves.

What do you know about the reality of ideas or about their role and their power? Nothing! Sometimes, you say, 'I had a splendid idea, today!' but you don't know that your idea was a spiritual being who came to visit you in the guise of an idea.[4] It was not just something vague and insubstantial that passed through your mind; it was an entity, a living creature and, instead of treasuring it, your reaction is often to say to yourself, 'What would my wife – or my friends or my children – say, if I accepted ideas of this kind?' Fear of what others might think opens the door to doubt and indecision, and when you drive out these bright entities, you are sapping your own energies, because the negative thoughts and feelings that take their place release substances into your bloodstream that have a congealing, constricting effect on you. Henceforth, my dear brothers and sisters, when you are visited by a luminous idea, take care to cleanse and purify yourselves so that it may put down roots in you and grow and bear magnificent fruit.[5]

A lot of people boast of having plenty of ideas. Yes, but if their ideas are only about how to obtain money or power, how to seduce women, etc., they are of no use to anyone. Many people are in a hurry to stifle any idea that does not concern money or material possessions and then, without realizing why, they find themselves in a perpetual state of uncertainty: they understand nothing of what goes on around them, their hearts and minds are empty, their will-power is undermined and debilitated. This condition is the direct result of the fact that they habitually drive out any luminous, divine idea that comes to them. You must realize that the invisible world sends us a ceaseless flow of luminous waves and spiritual influences, but that we cannot actually receive them unless we open ourselves to them. My wish for you is that these luminous waves may enter you and remain within you as seeds in your garden and that, in the years to come, all men may stroll in your garden and enjoy your ripe fruits.

Each human being is linked to thousands of other beings, both more advanced and less advanced than himself. If his thoughts and feelings are of a lofty nature, he can help those that are less advanced – animals, plants and the stones of the earth – for his own states of mind and soul and everything that he experiences, is transmitted to those below him and, as he is also linked to beings of a higher order, their divine energies begin to flow into him from that living, unbroken chain of life.

The wisdom, light and love of the angels and archangels are channelled, first of all, through the initiates and great masters before flooding our beings. But the tide of wisdom does not cease to flow once it reaches us; we, too, are channels through which it passes to plants and minerals and to all the lower levels of creation to which we are connected. Then, by means of another, upward current, these forces are swept up again, from the mineral kingdom to the highest levels of nature. As long as a man remains linked to this living chain of beings, the joy, peace and light of the initiates will flow through him.

And this is where the great danger lies for those who want to be independent and who think that, by setting themselves apart and isolating themselves from others, they will be better able to control and command men and events: they cut themselves off from this living chain of beings and, in doing so, cut themselves off from the sources of energy. No wonder, then, that they become vulnerable to every kind of misfortune or mishap. For where will they get the ideas, inspiration, wisdom and strength they need for their everyday life? 'They'll find it in themselves', you may say. Yes, for a month or a year, perhaps; but they will soon use up all their reserves. The bonds that bind them to a higher order of beings are destroyed by their pride and vanity and their determination to be independent, with the result that they lose any power they may have once had. Perhaps they had magnificent things in mind to begin with but, before long, those plans will come to nothing, for it is impossible to accomplish anything great if one's links with the living chain of creation have been severed. It is as though a light bulb refused to recognize that it was no more than a conductor, a vehicle, for the current from the power station and imagined that it was its own source of light.

The truth is that, whether we like it or not, we are connected, we do have bonds that bind us to beings of a higher order, but these unconscious bonds must become a conscious relationship if the living current is to flow in us. He who rejects or refuses to acknowledge this relationship eventually loses all light and strength. Man can be extremely powerful, he can work miracles, but he must never forget that he is nothing more than a vehicle for energies that come from above. He must constantly remind himself that it is divine wisdom that acts through him, that it is the divine world that manifests itself through him, otherwise he will lose everything. Even if someone has already been an initiate in the past, if he starts to believe that the source of his actions lies within himself, that everything depends solely on his own will, he will end by losing everything.

Brotherhood must exist in the world among men because it already exists in nature, and men must live according to the laws of nature. This Brotherhood that exists in the universe is what we call the Universal White Brotherhood and it is made up of all the great prophets, initiates and masters of humanity.[6] They all work together, like bees in a hive, preparing food for the Lord. If, today, men are unhappy and feel so isolated and cut off from each other, it is because their ties to the great masters have been cut. And you must realize that, in these conditions, it is impossible for a man to find his master. A master is a link in the great hierarchical chain of life and no one who has severed his ties with this hierarchy can hope to find his master. People may think that they have found a great many masters in America or Europe or Asia, but they are masters only outwardly; those who follow them are not yet living in the presence of an inner master.

How can you be sure of the inner presence of a master? How can you tell whether the voice you hear is really his? Anybody can say that he listens to his own inner master, but three conditions have to be fulfilled for this to be true. First, he must begin to see his way clearly and cease to stumble up against all kinds of obstacles. Second, he must begin to love all creatures and to feel his heart expanding with gratitude and brimming over with praise and thanksgiving. And, finally, his will must gradually free itself and become capable of accomplishing, unreservedly, all that is most noble and beautiful. If a man fulfils these three conditions, it does not matter whether he finds a master on the physical plane or not, for he has already found his inner master; it is this master who abides in him, who guides him and sets him free.

What is our relationship with those who are more advanced than ourselves? When we are travelling on a strange road, we feel safer and less lonely if we are with friends whose presence sustains and encourages us. It is reassuring to know that others are treading the same path and experiencing the same difficulties. Similarly, in a Brotherhood, we feel an increase of strength, faith and light; we benefit from the help and support and protection of others. And what of the relationship between ourselves and those who are less advanced? One day, thanks to them, we shall be blessed with quantities of friends. Suppose you have some pet cats: one day, in a future incarnation, they will become lovely young girls! And you, who may well be angels by then, will visit them and make friends with them!

One day you will see how many blessings are showered on you, thanks to the presence of the Brotherhood! You will continually feel yourselves becoming happier and stronger. The Brotherhood will be like a magnetic chain, a channel along which a stream of living water will flow for the nourishment of all creatures. All the sorrow, sadness and misfortunes we experience come from our being cut off from this living chain. This is why it is so important to devote at least a few minutes every day to thinking of this chain; from now on, try not to let a day go by without renewing this link. In this way you will be attuning yourselves to the harmonious vibrations of the Universal White Brotherhood, and all that the initiates experience, their freedom, their ecstasies and raptures, all the gems and riches they possess, will be communicated to you. For the initiates and great masters have no desire to keep these treasures to themselves, their one idea is to share them, at once, with others; if we are not receiving them it is because we are not part of that chain, or because we have not made ourselves ready to receive them. Every day, when he wakes up in the morning, he who is linked to this chain finds a gift waiting for him and, on opening it, he finds guidance, nourishment and treasures of all kinds. He can get up and go to work happy and confident because he has received these gifts. And those who wake up in the morning and find no gifts waiting for them, are unhappy: but it is their own fault. It is because they have failed to subscribe to the 'morning paper' in which the invisible world publishes the guidance warnings and encouragements each one of us needs. If you want to know happiness, joy and light, you must subscribe to this newspaper, and this means that you must pay something. Ah, that is something that is very hard to accept, isn't it? As soon as there is any mention of payment, everyone turns and runs! If something can be had for nothing, that is another matter; people come flocking! But if they have to pay, things are suddenly much more difficult! But this is precisely one of the things we have to learn: exactly the same principles apply in the invisible world as here, on earth. The only difference is that, instead of paying with money, we have to pay with thoughts of trust, patience, humility, love and hope.

We must give all our attention, all our love and all our good will to the Master of the Universal White Brotherhood, and he, in return, will send us strength, guidance and help. Yes, and you need not worry: he will always send it to the right address! But if we never give anything, we shall never receive anything either: in order to receive we have to give, and the more we give the more we receive. If you think that you can obtain whatever you want without an effort, without luminous thoughts and disinterested love, you will never know fulfilment for, even though you may obtain every material thing you ever wished for, such an attitude will always prevent you from discovering the meaning of life and you will never know happiness, light and freedom.

When I say that we have to give, this includes giving thanks. Yes, because heaven and the beings of the divine world never cease giving you things and you never even thank them. In any case, don't think that you can obtain anything very much without a great deal of work. All unconsciously, people calculate and try to cut corners, hoping to get substantial results with very little effort; they try to get what they want by trickery rather than by hard work. Unfortunately, all such calculations are useless in the face of reality; the entities of the higher worlds tell us that such methods are totally ineffectual. In the invisible world we find all that exists on earth, and this means that there are shops there, just as there are here. And the shopkeepers are very obliging; they give you whatever you want, but then they hold out their hands and expect to be paid. If you say that you thought you could have whatever you wanted for nothing, they will simply take it all away again. Of course, this is a manner of speaking for, to be accurate, it is not the invisible world that is built on the lines of the visible world, but just the opposite: it is the visible world that is built according to the laws of the invisible world and these laws are to be found on all levels and in every domain.

The more love you give, the more you receive. Sometimes, in fact, one can receive so much that it becomes almost unbearable. Exert yourselves, work hard to help others and set them free, so that the invisible world may free you and give you the strength you need to reach the summit. The road is long and very arduous; make no mistake about it. Those who claim that they can get to the top at once, in a month or two, are deceiving themselves and others. Some think that, after a few months, they are already true initiates, that they are in a position to instruct others, that they know all there is to know, that they are masters! This is not possible! One has to study, acquire a great deal of experience and practise for a very long time before being capable of instructing others and becoming a master. Anyone who is not already prepared must wait for centuries before he can teach others. You will say, 'But you have just told us that we should help others and set them free. You are contradicting yourself!' No, whatever level you may have reached, you can always teach what you already know. But what you must never do is try to teach what you do not know yourself, and what you are not yet capable of doing. If the blind lead the blind, both of them fall into the ditch. I have so often seen this already.

Personally, I do not claim to be a master.* For the time being I am simply teaching you what I have seen and heard from my own Master and what I have learned for myself in the twenty years spent at his side. But I never talk to you about something that I have not experienced and verified for myself. It is always

---

* This lecture was given in 1938. It was only in 1960, after his return from India, that Omraam Mikhaël Aïvanhov yielded to his disciples' insistence and allowed them to address him as Master. (Editor's note)

possible to help, enlighten and love others, as long as one does so on one's own level; it is not necessary to wait for centuries in order to do this. If you wait too long, everyone else will be dead before you have made up your mind to be useful! While others are falling into hell, it is not enough just to look on and tell them, 'I'm sorry, but I can't help you yet. I shall not be ready to do so for hundreds of years!' This is the language of idleness. On the other hand, those who think that, in the space of a few months, they can become masters and transform the whole world, are being presumptuous, and you should follow the example of neither!

The time has come for you to prepare the links which will bind you to the Universal White Brotherhood. The important thing is not that this Brotherhood should exist and its members meet frequently on the physical level, but that we should be linked to the Universal White Brotherhood that has already existed for thousands of years on the invisible level. The consequences of not being linked to the Universal White Brotherhood are extremely grave, for it means that the currents from above can no longer enter us to purify us and defend us from harmful elements. As a result of being cut off from those currents, we begin to be infested by inferior beings and the inevitable rot and sickening stench that always accompany them. If we refuse to allow the influences from above to enter us, it means that we are allowing quantities of matter from the lower levels to accumulate and stagnate in us and, eventually, to poison us. All our misfortunes are due to the presence within us of beings of a lower order that are never opposed or driven out by a purifying current from on high.[7]

When someone feels that these inferior beings are invading him and trampling his inner flower beds, stealing his treasure and snuffing out his inner light, it means that the links that bound him to the chain of the Universal White Brotherhood have not been strong enough. But he does not realize this; he complains, 'I don't know what's the matter with me. I feel unhappy and anxious... as though I were being torn apart.' Then he goes to see a doctor or tries to forget his troubles in a whirl of social activities, but to no avail, because he is full of these inferior beings. The only way he can be free of them is by restoring his ties to the creatures of the sublime world, by opening his heart and mind, his soul and spirit, and letting the blessed currents from above purify and nourish him and rescue him from all these baneful entities. When the currents from on high are very strong, these creatures cannot swim against the tide; it forces them back. If they do manage to get a foothold, it is because the current from above is not strong enough; in other words, we have been proud, distrustful and anarchic and have not cherished and strengthened our bond with the Universal White Brotherhood – also known as the White Lodge – of which Christ is the head.

Before it can manifest itself on the visible plane, the Brotherhood must live in our souls; in this way it will necessarily manifest itself, one day, in the visible world. I have no desire to build only a physical Brotherhood; that would be something purely superficial. The Brotherhood must be formed by the spontaneous coming together of souls. This is why I do not want to gather you together at once. I want to wait until the desire to learn more, the desire to sing and do spiritual exercises together, expresses itself spontaneously. Everything must be prepared gradually. We must begin by creating a living chain. I want to be sure that you know why you come here and that it is neither for me nor for each other, but for yourselves, because you are convinced that you receive great spiritual treasures here.

The more you give the more you receive. Don't come here for me; I don't need you. Heaven gives me all I need; if I want you to come here, it is in order to give to you. Don't be insulted by this; I love and respect you, but I want to get you to understand what a terrible mistake we make when we sacrifice our higher Self, our link with heaven and all the higher beings, for the opinion of a handful of very ordinary people. When we do that we are throwing away the kingdom of God, we are breaking off our

communication with the Universal White Brotherhood. As far
as I am concerned, I am interested in satisfying only your souls
and spirits; I refuse to satisfy anything else in you.

Remember that what matters above all else is to cherish your
ties with the great beings on high so that the currents from above
can continually flow through you and purify and illuminate you.
Fear, selfishness, distrust and the passions break the chain that
binds us to the higher world and open the door to noxious entities
from which no human being has the power to rescue us. Only
love, wisdom and truth can deliver us from the clutches of these
inferior beings.

The secret of life is hidden in gratitude, humility,[8] prayer[9]
and the link with beings of a higher order.[10] Oh, of course,
very few people are interested in these things; they are too
busy with problems that they think are far more important. If
you talk to people about love, they say that they have heard all
about it thousands of times already. If you tell them that they
must be humble, they think you are saying that they should be
mediocre and wishy-washy, and they declare that the clergy has
preached humility for far too long. That may be true, but they
don't realize that they have always looked at these things from
a purely theoretical point of view; they deal with everything on
the intellectual level and never make the slightest attempt to put
any of it into practice. Our teaching is not new, and yet it is new
because it is the practical application of all the great truths that
have been known to man for thousands of years. It provides us
with methods adapted to our times for the development of all
the divine qualities in man.* When we apply this teaching we
discover the meaning of life.

* I said that our teaching was not new, but I think that this point needs a little
clarification. All the spiritual teachings of the past were designed to help
individuals to reach perfection. The means that enabled men to travel, communicate and propagate their ideas were very restricted. Generally speaking,
each one was alone in seeking spiritual development and acquiring knowledge

There are many, nowadays, who claim to know what life is all about but who are not strong, happy people. It does not occur to them that true knowledge is incompatible with weakness, unhappiness, anxiety and fear. They see nothing abnormal in being extremely learned whilst behaving like an ignoramus! You must understand, henceforth, that the only unhappiness of those who really are sure of the meaning of life is the unhappiness of others; they feel other people's pain, but they communicate their own joy to them and take on their burdens. True initiates never suffer for personal reasons; they suffer for others. Anyone who thinks that he knows what life is all about, therefore, and who, in spite of that, feels unhappy, discouraged or depressed and disillusioned, is deceiving himself. He knows little or nothing about it or, at best, his understanding is misleading and purely theoretical. A true comprehension of the meaning of life brings with it an inner sensation too marvellous for words to describe.[11] And the only reason why the meaning of life remains hidden to men is that they do not put the great truths into practice in their own, individual lives.

---

and spiritual powers, and could, therefore, contribute only indirectly to the good of the whole. Men sought the kingdom of God, but as individuals; they worked for the salvation of their own souls. But nowadays, with the increasingly sophisticated means of locomotion and information at our disposal (planes, radio and television), conditions are no longer what they were, and the possibilities for achieving the kingdom of God are at hand; distance no longer exists, men can communicate with each other and spread their ideas from one corner of the earth to another. Unfortunately, the thing that has still not changed is the self-centred spirit of individualism and isolation. Inwardly, Brotherhood is neither understood nor practised, not only by those who work on the political level but even in the religious and spiritual teachings. Division, barriers, hostility and wars are rife, in every direction. Look at Ireland! The teaching of the Universal White Brotherhood is not a new science or a new philosophy; it is simply a new goal, a new trend, an ideal of collectivity and universality: all human beings are brothers and sisters, sons and daughters of the same heavenly Father and Mother, and they must be united like the cells of a single organism which all collaborate and work harmoniously together for the health and well-being of that organism. This is the new element that our teaching brings to the world. (Note added by Omraam Mikhaël Aïvanhov, October 1972)

Now that you know that this living hierarchy of beings exists, make sure that every one of your thoughts, feelings and acts is such as to keep you linked to it. Join yourselves to the chain of the Universal White Brotherhood so that you may pull yourselves up, step by step, until, one day, you reach the very top.

May light and peace be with you!

Sèvres, 10 July 1938

Notes
1. See *The Powers of Thought*, Izvor Coll. n° 224, chap. 5: 'How Thought Produces Material Results'.
2. See *Love Greater Than Faith*, Izvor Coll. n° 239, chap. 2: 'Destructive doubt: unification and bifurcation'.
3. See *The Yoga of Nutrition*, Izvor Coll. n° 204, chap. 5: 'Vegetarianism'.
4. See *The Powers of Thought*, Izvor Coll. n° 224, chap. 4: 'Thoughts are Living Beings'.
5. See *The Seeds of Happiness*, Izvor Coll. n° 231, chap. 19: 'The Garden of Souls and Spirits'.
6. See *The Fruits of The Tree of Life – The Cabbalistic Tradition*, Complete Works, vol. 32, chap. 19: 'The Glorified Souls'.
7. See *Life Force*, Complete Works, vol. 5, chap. 7: 'Unwanted Guests', and *'Au commencement était le Verbe' – commentaires des Évangiles*, Complete Works, vol. 9, chap. 12: 'Il y a plusieurs demeures dans la maison de mon Père'.
8. See *True Alchemy or the Quest for Perfection*, Izvor Coll. n° 221, chap. 11: 'Pride and Humility'.
9. See *La prière*, Brochure n° 305.
10. See *What is a Spiritual Master?*, Izvor Coll. n° 207, chap. 2: 'The Necessity for a Spiritual Master', and *Angels and other Mysteries of The Tree of Life*, Izvor Coll. n° 236.
11. See *The Seeds of Happiness*, Izvor Coll. n° 231, chap. 6: 'The Meaning of Life'.

BIBLICAL REFERENCES

Chapter 1
'No one can enter the kingdom of God without being born of water and Spirit' – *John 3: 5, p. 14, p. 17.*
Matter is opposed to the Spirit – *Matt. 26: 41, Letter of Paul to the Romans 7: 5-25 and 8: 2-6, p. 25.*

Chapter 2
'Ask, and it will be given to you' – *Luke 11: 9, pp. 41-42.*

Chapter 3
Jacob's Ladder – *Gen. 28: 12, p. 61.*
'If your eye is healthy' ' – *Matt. 6: 22, p. 62.*
'All is vanity' – *Ecclesiastes 1: 2, p. 68.*
Solomon: his seven hundred wives – *I Kings 11: 3, p. 69.*
'I am the way, the truth, and the life' – *John 14: 6, p. 69.*
Eve formed from one of Adam's ribs – *Gen. 2: 21, p. 76.*
Cain and Abel – *Gen. 4: 1-2, p. 76.*

Chapter 4
'Anyone who hears my word' – *John 5: 24-25, p. 81.*
'They have ears but do not hear' – *Jeremiah 5: 21, p. 82.*
'Those who have ears to hear, let them hear' – *Matt. 11: 15, 13: 9 and 43, Mark 4: 9, Luke 8: 8 and 14: 35, p. 82.*
'Let anyone who has an ear listen to what the Spirit is saying to the churches' – *Revelation 2: 11, 17, 29, etc., p. 82.*
'You may freely eat of every tree of the garden' – *Gen. 2: 16, p. 87.*
'Your will be done, on earth as it is in heaven' – *Matt. 6: 10, p. 88.*
Elijah flees from Jezebel – *I Kings 19: 1-9, p. 99.*
God speaks to Elijah in a still, small voice – *I Kings 19: 11-13, p. 99.*
'Go at once to Nineveh' – *Jonas 1: 2, p. 99.*
'Prophesy to these bones' – *Ezekiel 37: 4-14, p. 101.*
'Do not be astonished at this' – *John 5: 28, p. 102.*

Books by Omraam Mikhaël Aïvanhov
(translated from the French)

Complete Works

Volume   1 – The Second Birth
Volume   2 – Spiritual Alchemy
Volume   5 – Life Force
Volume   6 – Harmony
Volume   7 – The Mysteries of Yesod
Volume 10 – The Splendour of Tiphareth
                    The Yoga of the Sun
Volume 11 – The Key to the Problems of Existence
Volume 12 – Cosmic Moral Law
Volume 13 – A New Earth
                    Methods, Exercises, Formulas, Prayers
Volume 14 – Love and Sexuality (Part I)
Volume 15 – Love and Sexuality (Part II)
Volume 16 – Hrani Yoga
                    The Alchemical and Magical Meaning of Nutrition
Volume 17 – 'Know Thyself' Jnana Yoga (Part I)
Volume 18 – 'Know Thyself' Jnana Yoga (Part II)
Volume 25 – A New Dawn:
                    Society and Politics in the Light of Initiatic Science (Part I)
Volume 26 – A New Dawn:
                    Society and Politics in the Light of Initiatic Science (Part II)
Volume 29 – On the Art of Teaching (Part III)
Volume 30 – Life and Work in an Initiatic School
                    Training for the Divine
Volume 32 – The Fruits of the Tree of Life
                    The Cabbalistic Tradition

Brochures

301 – The New Year
302 – Meditation
303 – Respiration
304 – Death and the Life Beyond
323 – Sunrise Meditations

By the same author:
(Translated from the French)

Izvor Collection

World Wide - Editor-Distributor
Editions Prosveta S.A. - Z.A. Le Capitou - B.P. 12
F - 83601 Fréjus CEDEX (France)
Tel. (33) 04 94 19 33 33 – Fax (33) 04 94 19 33 34
Web: www.prosveta.com – e-mail: international@prosveta.com

Distributors

AUSTRALIA
PROSVETA Australia – P.O. Box 538 – Mittagong – N.S.W. 2575 Australia
Tel. (61) (0) 2 4855 0189 – Fax. (61) (0) 2 4872 2641 – e-mail: prosveta.au@bigpond.com

AUSTRIA
HARMONIEQUELL VERSAND – Hof 37 – A- 5302 Henndorf am Wallersee
Tel. / fax (43) 6214 7413 – e-mail: info@prosveta.at

BELGIUM & LUXEMBOURG
PROSVETA BENELUX – Beeldenmakersstraat 1 – B 8000 Brugge
Tel./Fax. (32)(0)50/61 69 10 – e-mail: prosveta@skynet.be
N.V. MAKLU Somersstraat 13-15 – B-2000 Antwerpen
Tel. (32) 3/231 29 00 – Fax (32) 3/233 26 59
S.D.L. CARAVELLE S.A. – rue du Pré aux Oies, 303 – 1130 Bruxelles
Tel. (32) 2 240 93 00 – Fax (32) 2 216 35 98
e-mail: info@sdlcaravelle.com

BOLIVIA
BELTRÁN – Calle Muñoz Cornejo, Sopocachi – La Paz
e-mail: mariabelre@yahoo.es

BULGARIA
SVETOGLED – Bd Saborny 16 A, appt 11 – 9000 Varna
e-mail: vassil100@abv.bg – Tel/Fax: (359) 52 63 90 94

CANADA
PROSVETA Inc. – 3950, Albert Mines – Canton-de-Hatley (Qc), J0B 2C0
Tel. (819) 564-8212 – Fax. (819) 564-1823 – *in Canada,* call toll free: 1-800-854-8212
e-mail: prosveta@prosveta-canada.com / www.prosveta-canada.com

COLOMBIA
PROSVETA COLOMBIA
Calle 174 Número 54B – 50 Interior 6 – Villa del Prado – Bogotá
Tel. (57 1) 6 14 53 85 / 6 72 16 89 – Fax. (57 1) 6 33 58 03
Celular: (57) 311 8 10 25 42 – e-mail: kalagiya@hotmail.com

CONGO
PROSVETA CONGO – 29, Avenue de la Révolution – B.P. 768 – Pointe-Noire
Tel.: (242) 948156 / (242) 5531254 – Fax: (242) 948156
e-mail: prosvetacongo@yahoo.fr

CYPRUS
THE SOLAR CIVILISATION BOOKSHOP – BOOKBINDING
73 D Kallipoleos Avenue – Lycavitos – P. O. Box 24947, 1305 – Nicosia
e-mail: heavenlight@primehome.com – Tel / Fax 00357-22-377503

CZECH REPUBLIC
PROSVETA – Ant. Sovy 18 – České Budejovice 370 05
Tel / Fax: (420) 38-53 10 227 – e-mail: prosveta@iol.cz

FRANCE – DOM TOM
Editions Prosveta S.A. - B.P. 12 – F - 83601 Fréjus CEDEX (France)
Tel. (33) 04 94 19 33 33 – Fax (33) 04 94 19 33 34
e-mail: international@prosveta.com – www.prosveta.com

GERMANY
PROSVETA Verlag GmbH – Heerstrasse 55 – 78628 Rottweil
Tel. (49) 741-46551 – Fax. (49) 741-46552 – e-mail: prosveta7@aol.com

GREAT BRITAIN – IRELAND
PROSVETA – The Doves Nest, Duddleswell Uckfield – East Sussex TN 22 3JJ
Tel. (44) (01825) 712988 – Fax (44) (01825) 713386 – e-mail: prosveta@pavilion.co.uk
GREECE
PYRINOS KOSMOS – BOOK - PUBLISHERS
16 Hippocratous Str., 106 80 ATHENS
Tel. 30/1/3602883, 30/1/3615233 – Fax : 30/1/3611234
e-mail : info@pyrinoskosmos.gr – www.pyrinoskosmos.gr
HAITI
PROSVETA DÉPÔT HAITI – Angle rue Faustin 1er et rue Bois Patate #25 bis
6110 Port-au-Prince
Tel. (509) 245 06 43 – Mobile: (509) 464 80 88 – e-mail: rbaaudant@yahoo.com
HOLLAND
STICHTING PROSVETA NEDERLAND – Zeestraat 50 – 2042 LC Zandvoort
Tel. (31) 33 25 345 75 – Fax. (31) 33 25 803 20 – e-mail: prosveta@worldonline.nl
ISRAEL
Zohar, P.B. 1046, Netanya 42110 – e-mail: prosveta.il@hotmail.com
ITALY
PROSVETA Coop. a r.l.
Casella Postale 55 – 06068 Tavernelle (PG)
Tel. (39) 075-835 84 98 – Fax (39) 075-6306 20 18 – e-mail: prosveta@tin.it
IVORY COAST
Librairie Prosveta – 25 rue Paul Langevin Zone 4C – 01 Abidjan
e-mail: prosvetafrique@yahoo.fr – Tel/Fax: (225) 21 25 42 11
LEBANON
PROSVETA LIBAN – P.O. Box 90-995
Jdeidet-el-Metn, Beirut – Tel. (03) 448560 – e-mail: prosveta_lb@terra.net.lb
NEW ZEALAND
PROSVETA NEW ZEALAND LTD
Unit 2, 212 Riddell Road – Glendowie – Auckland
Tel. (64) 9 889 0805 or (64) 27 356 0107 – e-mail: info@prosveta.co.nz
NORWAY
PROSVETA NORDEN – Postboks 318, N-1502 Moss
Tel. (47) 69 26 51 40 – Fax (47) 69 26 51 08 – e-mail: info@prosveta.no
PORTUGAL
EDIÇÕES PROSVETA
Rua Palmira 66 r/c - C – 1170 - 287 Lisboa
Tel. / Fax (351) 213 540 764 – e-mail: prosvetapt@hotmail.com
ROMANIA
ANTAR – Str. N. Constantinescu 10 – Bloc 16A - sc A - Apt. 9 – Sector 1 – 71253 Bucarest
Tel. 004021-231 28 78 – Tel./ Fax 004021-231 37 19
e-mail : prosveta_ro@yahoo.com
RUSSIA
EDITIONS PROSVETA
143 964 Moskovskaya oblast, g. Reutov – 4, post/box 4
Tel./ Fax (495) 525 18 17 – Tél. (495) 795 70 74 – e-mail: prosvetarus@gmail.com
SPAIN
ASOCIACIÓN PROSVETA ESPAÑOLA – C/ Ausias March n° 23 Ático
SP-08010 Barcelona – Tel (34) (93) 412 31 85 – Fax (34) (93) 318 89 01
e-mail: aprosveta@prosveta.es
UNITED STATES
PROSVETA US Dist.
29781 Shenandoah LN – Canyon Country CA 91387
Tel. (661) 252-9090
e-mail: prosveta-usa@earthlink.net. / www.prosveta-usa.com

SWITZERLAND
PROSVETA Société Coopérative
Ch. de la Céramone 2 – CH - 1808 Les Monts-de-Corsier
Tel. (41) 21 921 92 18 – Fax. (41) 21 922 92 04
e-mail: prosveta@bluewin.ch
VENEZUELA
PROSVETA VENEZUELA C. A. – Calle Madrid
Edificio La Trinidad – Las Mercedes – Caracas D.F.
Tel. (58) 414 134 75 34 – e-mail: prosvetavenezuela@gmail.com

*Updated list 16.02.09. If you cannot contact one of these distributors,
consult the internet site www.prosveta.com*

The aim of the Universal White Brotherhood association
is the study and practice of the Teaching
of Master Omraam Mikhaël Aïvanhov,
published and distributed
by Prosveta.
All enquiries about the association should be addressed
to:
Universal White Brotherhood
The Doves Nest, Duddleswell, Uckfield
East Sussex TN22 3JJ, GREAT BRITAIN
Tel: (44) (0)1825 712150 – Fax: (44) (0)1825 713386
E-mail: uwb@pavilion.co.uk

Printed in March 2009
by Présence Graphique
37260 Monts – France

Dépôt légal: Mars 2009
1ᵉʳ dépôt légal dans la même collection: 1988